Microwave Magic
Cooking for Health II

Grolier Limited
TORONTO

Contributors to this series:

Recipes and Technical Assistance:
École de cuisine Bachand-Bissonnette
Cooking consultants:
Denis Bissonnette
Michèle Émond
Dietician:
Christiane Barbeau
Photos:
Laramée Morel Communications
Audio-Visuelles
Design:
Claudette Taillefer
Assistants:
Julie Deslauriers
Philippe O'Connor
Joan Pothier
Accessories:
Andrée Cournoyer
Writing:
Communications La Griffe Inc.
Text Consultants:
Cap et bc inc.
Advisors:
Roger Aubin
Joseph R. De Varennes
Gaston Lavoie
Kenneth H. Pearson

Assembly:
Carole Garon
Vital Lapalme
Jean-Pierre Larose
Carl Simmons
Gus Soriano
Marc Vallières
Production Managers:
Gilles Chamberland
Ernest Homewood
Production Assistants:
Martine Gingras
Catherine Gordon
Kathy Kishimoto
Peter Thomlison
Art Director:
Bernard Lamy
Editors:
Laurielle Ilacqua
Susan Marshall
Margaret Oliver
Robin Rivers
Lois Rock
Jocelyn Smyth
Donna Thomson
Dolores Williams
Development:
Le Groupe Polygone Éditeurs Inc.

We wish to thank the following firms, PIER I IMPORTS and LE CACHE POT, for their contribution to the illustration of this set.

The series editors have taken every care to ensure that the information given is accurate. However, no cookbook can guarantee the user successful results. The editors cannot accept any responsibility for the results obtained by following the recipes and recommendations given.

Canadian Cataloguing in Publication Data

Main entry under title:

Cooking for Health II

(Microwave magic ; 21)
Translation of: La Cuisine santé II.
Includes index.
ISBN 0-7172-2442-2

1. Cookery (Natural foods).   2. Microwave cookery.
I. Series: Microwave magic (Toronto, Ont.) ; 21.

TX832.C873 1988   641.5'637   C88-094220-7

Contents

Microwave Magic is a multi-volume set, with each volume devoted to a particular type of cooking. So, if you are looking for a chicken recipe, you simply go to one of the two volumes that deal with poultry. Each volume has its own index, and the final volume contains a general index to the complete set.

Microwave Magic puts over twelve hundred recipes at your fingertips. You will find it as useful as the microwave oven itself. Enjoy!

Note from the Editor

How to Use this Book

The books in this set have been designed to make your job as easy as possible. As a result, most of the recipes are set out in a standard way.

We suggest that you begin by consulting the information chart for the recipe you have chosen. You will find there all the information you need to decide if you are able to make it: preparation time, cost per serving, level of difficulty, number of calories per serving and other relevant details. Thus, if you have only 30 minutes in which to prepare the evening meal, you will quickly be able to tell which recipe is possible and suits your schedule.

The list of ingredients is always clearly separated from the main text. When space allows, the ingredients are shown together in a photograph so that you can make sure you have them all without rereading the list—

another way of saving your valuable time. In addition, for the more complex recipes we have supplied photographs of the key stages involved either in preparation or serving.

All the dishes in this book have been cooked in a 700 watt microwave oven. If your oven has a different wattage, consult the conversion chart that appears on the following page for cooking times in different types of oven. We would like to emphasize that the cooking times given in the book are a minimum. If a dish does not seem to be cooked enough, you may return it to the oven for a few more minutes. Also, the cooking time can vary according to your ingredients: their water and fat content, thickness, shape and even where they come from. We have therefore left a blank space on each recipe page in which you can note

the cooking time that suits you best. This will enable you to add a personal touch to the recipes that we suggest and to reproduce your best results every time.

Although we have put all the technical information together at the front of this book, we have inserted a number of boxed entries called **MICROTIPS** throughout to explain particular techniques. They are brief and simple, and will help you obtain successful results in your cooking.

With the very first recipe you try, you will discover just how simple microwave cooking can be and how often it depends on techniques you already use for cooking with a conventional oven. If cooking is a pleasure for you, as it is for us, it will be all the more so with a microwave oven. Now let's get on with the food.

The Editor

Key to the Symbols

For ease of reference, the following symbols have been used on the recipe information charts.

The pencil symbol is a reminder to write your cooking time in the space provided.

Level of Difficulty

Easy

Moderate

Complex

Cost per Serving

$ Inexpensive

$ $ Moderate

$ $ $ Expensive

Power Levels

All the recipes in this book have been tested in a 700 watt oven. As there are many microwave ovens on the market with different power levels, and as the names of these levels vary from one manufacturer to another, we have decided to give power levels as a percentage. To adapt the power levels given here, consult the chart opposite and the instruction manual for your oven.

Generally speaking, if you have a 500 watt or 600 watt oven you should increase cooking times by about 30% over those given, depending on the actual length of time required. The shorter the original cooking time, the greater the percentage by which it must be lengthened. The 30% figure is only an average. Consult the chart for detailed information on this topic.

Power Levels

HIGH: 100% - 90%	Vegetables (except boiled potatoes and carrots) Soup Sauce Fruits Browning ground beef Browning dish Popcorn
MEDIUM HIGH: 80% - 70%	Rapid defrosting of precooked dishes Muffins Some cakes Hot dogs
MEDIUM: 60% - 50%	Cooking tender meat Cakes Fish Seafood Eggs Reheating Boiled potatoes and carrots
MEDIUM LOW: 40%	Cooking less tender meat Simmering Melting chocolate
DEFROST: 30% **LOW: 30% - 20%**	Defrosting Simmering Cooking less tender meat
WARM: 10%	Keeping food warm Allowing yeast dough to rise

Cooking Time Conversion Chart

700 watts	**600 watts***
5 s	11 s
15 s	20 s
30 s	40 s
45 s	1 min
1 min	1 min 20 s
2 min	2 min 40 s
3 min	4 min
4 min	5 min 20 s
5 min	6 min 40 s
6 min	8 min
7 min	9 min 20 s
8 min	10 min 40 s
9 min	12 min
10 min	13 min 30 s
20 min	26 min 40 s
30 min	40 min
40 min	53 min 40 s
50 min	66 min 40 s
1 h	1 h 20 min

* There is very little difference in cooking times between 500 watt ovens and 600 watt ovens.

Nutrition: Science and Good Taste

It is unlikely that there is anyone among your acquaintances who is seriously worried about not having food on the table tomorrow. Generally speaking, an abundance of food is available to North Americans and the only problem they face is deciding what they would most enjoy eating at mealtime.

Does Food in Abundance Guarantee Good Health?

In supermarkets, we find a splendid array of fresh foods: different types of meat, exquisite cheeses and brightly colored fruits and vegetables. These basic ingredients can be turned into everyday meals or splendid feasts. Some are produced in Canada. Others are imported from countries all over the world—Gouda cheese from Holland, artichokes from California, papayas from the Caribbean, rice from Southeast Asia and so on. The list is endless.

Another luxury we take for granted is that we are able, for the most part, to buy all these different foods throughout the year. The food industry has found ingenious ways to keep supplies continuous. Some out-of-season foods, such as strawberries, are available frozen. Others, such as peas and beans, are canned, and still others, such as dates and apricots, are dried.

However, this abundance of food does not in itself guarantee good health. Eating well does not mean eating whatever you want when you feel hungry; it means basing your eating habits on scientific principles and not on instinct. Nutritionists have established some simple guidelines to help us choose the right foods. In a way, you should think of your kitchen as a nutrition laboratory where you can experiment with different combinations of foods to get the formula just right—the formula for a balanced diet.

Quantity . . . or Quality?

It is possible to be undernourished without being emaciated. In fact, a person may be seriously obese and yet remain undernourished in clinical terms. An example of this might be a fifteen-year-old who routinely skips breakfast and has a bag of potato chips, a chocolate bar and a soft drink for lunch, followed by a hamburger and a chocolate milk shake for supper. This diet, conspicuously lacking in fresh fruits and vegetables as well as in other nutritious foods, is low in dietary fiber and rich in empty calories. In a short time, this teenager would be overweight and would probably suffer from blemished skin and other health problems associated with poor nutrition. The same person, however, would not suffer from hunger.

Good health is linked to a healthy and varied diet, one that provides the body with all the nutrients it needs—proteins, vitamins, minerals and trace elements. If you follow the advice given in *Health Cookery II,* you will be taking an important step in the right direction.

The Right Balance

There are countless so-called miracle diets that promise radiant good health. Fasting, Zen, vegetarianism and the grapefruit diet are only some of the many diets that have been proposed for good health. These diets can be very complex or, some of them, downright bizarre. However, for most people, all that is required to maintain good health is a simple, well-balanced diet.

The concept of a balanced diet is perfectly straightforward. Only a few basic principles need to be understood, two of the keys being quality and variety. You should choose foods each day from the four main food groups outlined by the Canadian Food Guide. These four groups are milk and dairy products; meat, fish, poultry and alternates; bread and cereals; and fruits and vegetables—all of which are full of vitamins and other nutrients essential to good health. There is no single food that has miraculous properties; no one food contains all the nutrients the body needs. One cup of broccoli contains a great deal of Vitamin A but has only half the calcium that you would get from the same amount of yoghurt. Both have a place in the daily diet.

Dare to Experiment

It is a good idea to try foods that are new to you. You probably know, for example, that a glass of orange juice is an excellent source of Vitamin C, but do you know that a medium papaya contains the same amount? Of course, you should do a little homework before trying every new food you come across. It is important to find out what nutrients it contains.

Some foods provide far more nutrients than others. For example, one ounce of Edam cheese contains 7.7 grams of protein and 7.8 grams of fat. Ten large olives, which have the same fat content, lack the protein. This is not to say that you should give up olives. There is no doubt that they are delicious, particularly when they are plump and ripe. However, if you decide to lose weight, you might recall their fat content and conquer your impulse to buy every type of olive available in the new Greek store in your neighborhood!

The Body's Essential Functions

The body is like a giant corporation in which the personnel are assigned to one of four essential functions:
- the fat and carbohydrate team, which provides the energy required for daily activities;
- the protein team, which is responsible for building and maintaining body tissue and fighting infection;
- the mineral team (see the chart of page 12), which looks after the infrastructure (the bones, teeth, muscles, nerves and blood);
- the vitamin team (see the chart on page 11, opposite), which deals with supplies and transports nutrients to those points where they are needed to keep the body in good working order.

There are three basic rules that must be followed so that each of these four teams can function without a hitch:
1. Each team must have a certain variety of foods to ensure that it has the supplies it needs.
2. The consumption of fat, alcohol and salt must be kept to a moderate level so that the teams can work without hindrance and remain less

likely to break down.
3. There must be a balance between the intake of food calories and the expenditure of energy so that the corporation does not find itself with a surplus that it cannot easily dispose of.

The Canadian Food Guide

The Canadian Food Guide provides very helpful advice on how to maintain a healthy, balanced diet. It sets out guidelines on choosing the right combinations of food in the right quantities, thereby achieving the correct balance of nutrients and calories. The guide classifies foods in four major groups: milk and dairy products; meat, fish, poultry and alternates; bread and cereals; and fruits and vegetables.

You simply include the right quantity of foods from each of these groups in your diet each day, and you are well on the way to good health!

The Canadian Food Guide: Recommended Daily Intake

Milk and Dairy Products
Children up to age 11:
2 to 3 servings
Asolescents:
3 to 4 servings
Pregnant women and nursing mothers:
3 to 4 servings
Adults:
2 servings

Standard Servings:
250 mL (1 cup) milk
175 mL (3/4 cup) yoghurt
45 g (1-1/2 oz) cheddar cheese

Meat, Fish, Poultry and Alternates
2 servings

Standard Servings
60 to 90 g (2 to 3 oz) lean meat, fish, poultry or liver, cooked
60 mL (4 tablespoons) peanut butter
60 g (2 oz) cheddar cheese
2 eggs
250 mL (1 cup) legumes

Some Essential Vitamins

Name	Function
Vitamin A (retinol)	— helps form strong bones and teeth — keeps the skin and mucous membranes in good condition
Vitamin B_1 (thiamin)	— aids growth and helps maintain a healthy appetite
Vitamin B_2 (riboflavin)	— keeps the eyes and skin healthy — keeps the nervous system in good condition
Vitamin B_3 (niacin)	— ensures normal growth and development
Vitamin B_6 (pyridoxine)	— is essential to the functioning of the brain — helps control the nervous system
Vitamin B_{12} (cobalamin)	— helps in the formation of red blood cells — protects the tissues found in the nervous system and in the gastrointestinal system — prevents anemia
Vitamin C (ascorbic acid)	— helps maintain healthy teeth and gums — helps maintain blood vessels
Vitamin D (calciferol)	— ensures strong teeth and bones — aids in calcium absorption
Vitamin E (tocopherol)	— slows down the aging process

Bread and Cereals
3 to 5 servings

Standard Servings
1 slice of bread
125 (1/2 cup) cooked cereal
1 muffin
125 mL (1/2 cup) cooked pasta
1/2 hamburger bun

Fruits and Vegetables
4 to 5 servings, of which two should be vegetables

Standard Servings
125 mL (1/2 cup) fruits or vegetables
125 (1/2 cup) fruit or vegetable juice
1 medium-sized potato, banana, orange or peach

Some Essential Minerals

Name	Function
Calcium	— helps form strong bones and teeth — keeps the nervous system in good condition — aids the normal blood-clotting process
Iron	— is essential to the formation of red blood cells
Iodine	— keeps the thyroid gland in good condition
Magnesium	— helps maintain strong bones and teeth — contributes to tissue development — helps the body to assimilate food energy
Phosphorus	— helps maintain strong bones and teeth
Zinc	— contributes to tissue development — helps the body to assimilate food energy

MICROTIPS

Beans Unlimited . . .

At the time of the Great Crash in 1929, needy families in Canada could not afford to buy meat and they consumed dry legumes, or pulses, as their major source of protein. This fact probably explains why these foods are not very popular today. But lima beans, kidney beans, green lentils and chick peas, to name but a few, certainly deserve a place in any larder. Legumes can be prepared in a thousand and one ways; they can be used to make healthy soups, salads, spread and casseroles. Small quantities of legumes can be added to some of your favorite recipes to supply extra nutrients. Don't forget that when they are combined with certain breads and cereals such as whole wheat bread or rice, legumes provide complete proteins.

A Healthy Life: What is the Right Approach?

In previous generations women spent hours kneading bread and cooking in overheated kitchens. When, in recent years, the food processing industry offered an alternative way of living, consumers rejoiced. Never before had it been possible to buy peas shelled, cleaned, precooked and sometimes flavored with butter in a ready-to-serve dish! And then there were the cakes that could be put together in no time by adding water, an egg and sometimes butter to a mixture that was neatly packaged. But after an initial wave of enthusiasm, disenchantment set in. During the 1970s people came to discover that these processed foods provided few nutrients; most were full of chemical additives, such as colors and preservatives, which could not be guaranteed to be harmless. Consumers began to think not only in terms of convenience but also in terms of nutrutional value and started to question the use of processed foods. They wanted good food again but they did not want cooking to be the burden it once was.

Hunger, Food Preferences . . . and Health

To eat properly it is important to understand what different types of food your body requires. Not being aware of these requirements can easily result in the selection of foods that are not good for you. You may neglect valuable foods thinking you are eating properly. Your hunger will be satisfied but in fact you will have eaten nothing but empty calories. Hunger is a clear sign that it is time to eat, but a full stomach is no guarantee of good health. Stuffing yourself with doughnuts or even drinking a liter of water very quickly will give you a sensation of fullness, but this feeling of satisfaction will not last. The body does not appreciate such excesses.

Individual food preferences are a poor guide when it comes to choosing the right foods. Common sense tells us that eating only our favorite foods will not keep us healthy. You can learn to like foods by trying them prepared in different ways. How many stories have you heard about children refusing to eat vegetables? If a child refuses to eat overcooked, tasteless vegetables, try him or her on broccoli cooked so that it is still slightly crunchy, with sliced almonds—and watch the change in attitude.

Decisions, Decisions

Because food is available to us in abundance, it can be difficult to choose just what to buy. Think about vegetables, for example. Once, you could only buy corn on its cob; nowadays, it can be bought frozen, canned, as whole kernels or cream style, puffed, washed, dried and so on. You can also, if you wish, buy vitamin pills containing all the vitamins that you would get from fresh corn. No wonder lovers of good food despair.

Making the Right Choices

The body needs all the different nutrients that come from each of the food groups. For this reason, it is important to include them all in a balanced diet, and not to eat too much of one and none of another. Variety, moderation and balance are the key words to bear in mind for a healthy diet. Also, along with proper food, physical exercise, the right amount of sleep and a positive outlook on life all contribute to good health—and allow you to indulge a little from time to time.

Alcohol and Diet

Alcohol is a sugar. It contains many calories and few nutrients. You should therefore consume it only in moderation. For example, a glass of wine provides as much food energy as a blueberry muffin but almost no food fiber. Worse, alcohol can spoil your appetite and prevent nutrients from being absorbed; many nutrients and minerals in food are lost because alcohol causes them to be discharged into the urine. As well, excessive alcohol intake can destroy the liver and harm both the brain and the heart. Finally, it can alter mood and behavior and slow the reflexes. In short, you cannot expect to drink a large amount of alcohol on a regular basis and remain healthy.

Good health is priceless. Proper food, sufficient exercise, restorative sleep, minimal stress and a good sense of humor combine to provide your best assurance of a balanced, healthy life.

Therapeutic Diets

Is your body suffering from too much salt, fat or sugar? There are diets that correct such health problems by restricting your intake of certain foods. You must watch your diet carefully, exercise patience and show a great deal of self-discipline if you want to get results. On the following pages you will find tips for each type of diet. Take careful note!

Low-Salt Diet

Salt, or sodium, is essential to life. However, numerous studies have established a link between consumption of salt (sodium chloride) and high blood pressure. As a result, doctors usually recommend a low-salt diet for people who suffer from high blood pressure. Besides, salt causes the body to retain water. Watch what happens when you sprinkle eggplant or cucumber with salt to remove the bitterness in their taste: the water in the vegetable is drawn toward the salt crystals. As processed foods frequently contain a large quantity of salt, even people who are healthy should not eat them too frequently. Always check the labels on food!

Deal with the Problem at its Source
Add only a little salt to food when you are cooking it. In most cases, you will be delighted to rediscover the real taste of various foods.

Do Not "Pass the Salt"

Taste the food on your plate before you add salt to it. Try not to add any. If possible, don't even put the salt on the table. In other words, don't pass the salt—pass *on* the salt.

Look for Salt Substitutes!

Find natural, healthy alternatives to salt. Try herbs, spices or lemon juice, which subtly enhance the flavor of many foods.

Check Before You Buy

Who has the willpower to eat just one potato chip? With this in mind, limit your purchases of salty foods such as chips, pretzels, pork products, smoked meats, salted nuts, commercial sauces and dressings and salted crackers. Read the labels carefully and choose products that contain only a little salt, baking powder, monosodium glutamate or any additive that includes the word "sodium."

Low-Calorie Diet

The golden rule if you want to lose a little of that extra weight is this: eat less and exercise more! It may be easy to say and not so easy to do, but you can do it if you follow these guidelines.

Select Your Food Carefully

Take the time to select low-calorie foods. A soft drink, for example, contains 100 calories while the same amount of vegetable juice has only 50.

Deal Effectively with Sudden Cravings

Cut down on snacks. If you feel you absolutely must eat, at least take measures to avoid chocolate bars and other foods that are high in calories. Try a box of raisins (just one!) or a piece of fresh fruit.

Save Dessert for Later

If you find yourself reaching for a snack during the afternoon or evening, even after a good meal, don't eat dessert at lunchtime or at supper. Instead, have a healthy snack such as fresh fruit, fruit juice or cubes of cheese, when you feel the need to eat.

Use Technology to Help Stay Trim

Use your microwave oven as often as possible because microwave cooking requires very little extra fat. It also enables you to prepare vegetables without losing any of their flavor and very little of their nutrients, so you won't be as tempted to add sauce or butter.

Choose Low-Calorie Options

A poached egg contains 75 calories; the same egg, fried, contains 115. Herbal tea, taken plain, or tea with lemon has no calories; a cup of coffee with cream and sugar has 60. Is the difference in taste really worth the extra rolls of fat?

Trick Your Stomach

Instead of heading toward the refrigerator when you feel a pang of hunger, pour yourself a large glass of water. The drink will temporarily satisfy your appetite as well as rehydrate your system.

Fool Yourself!

Try serving your meals on small plates rather than on large ones. You will be fooled into thinking you are having a larger meal than you really are because the plate is full.

Take the time to eat slowly. Mealtimes will last longer and you won't be consuming extra calories. Have a relaxing bath before bedtime rather than a snack—much better for your figure!

Avoid Weight Fluctuation

If you overeat for even a short period, you will quickly put on weight. In the same way, however, once you stop these bad habits you will lose weight with little or no effort.

Consult the chart on page 16 for small but effective tips on how to keep your weight from fluctuating.

Give Up:	You Will Lose:
1 square of butter or margarine each day	2.2 kg (5 lb) in one year
1 slice of bread each day	2.7 kg (6 lb) in one year
1 doughnut each week	1 kg (2.2 lb) in one year
10 potato chips each week	0.7 kg (1.5 lb) in one year
1 glass of pop each week	0.5 kg (1.1 lb) in one year

MICROTIPS

Preserving the Vitamins in Vegetables

Do not leave vegetables at room temperature for longer than absolutely necessary. Even in the refrigerator, they will lose most of their Vitamin C within 3 or 4 days.

Whenever possible, scrape or brush vegetables and cook them unpeeled. Because much of the vitamin content is found close to the surface, you can lose one tenth of it when you peel them. If you really find the skin inedible, remove it once the vegetable has been cooked; it will then come away easily, with the result that you lose fewer vitamins.

Cut vegetables into as few pieces as possible; the smaller you cut the pieces, the more vitamins they lose. If you must cut them, do so after cooking them.

Keep the cooking water and use it as stock for soups or sauces. Add some of it to the milk in a cream sauce; the resulting sauce will be lighter and more nutritious.

Avoid soaking vegetables in water; some of the vitamins and all the mineral salts are water soluble and are therefore lost in the process.

Low-Sugar Diet

Natural sugars, such as those found in fruits and vegetables, are usually well tolerated by the body. The same cannot be said for refined sugar, which poses an enormous health risk. At the beginning of our century, when life has put more physical demands on most people, the average consumption of sugar per person per year was about 40 pounds. Today, that figure has doubled. As a result, the average North American consumes nearly 500 calories per day in sugar. Many people, such as diabetics, must avoid concentrated sugar. But everyone is at risk from eating too much sugar. Here are a few tips to help you cut down.

Look for Hidden Sugar!
Beware of sugar in desserts, soft drinks, sweetened cereals and in canned fruit syrup. Steer clear of jams, molasses, sweetened chewing gum, fruit drinks, flavored yoghurts and jello powder.

If It's Sweet, It's Sugar
Honey, molasses and brown sugar are sugar to the same extent as the refined white product, and they do not contain significant quantities of other nutrients. The same reasoning can be applied in some degree to fruits; although they do contain valuable nutrients, you should not overindulge. Sugar is still sugar.

Get Off to a Good Start
If you want to avoid the temptation of tucking into a sugary snack about 11 A.M., be sure to eat a good, nourishing breakfast, one that will leave you feeling satisfied until lunchtime. Top your morning cereal with fresh fruit and steer clear of toast and jam. The latter may be delicious, but it contains far too much concentrated sugar.

Digestion: The Chemistry of Life

The body uses the foods we eat as its building materials, breaking them down and recombining them in ways that enable tissues to renew themselves and the body to remain in good working order. The digestive system employs a combination of mechanical and chemical processes to break foods down so that the nutrients they contain can be put to use. The first step in digestion involves the mechanical process of chewing. The saliva in the mouth is combined with the food to break it down to a pulp, which then makes its way down the esophagus by a wave of muscle contractions to the stomach. In the stomach, the food is further broken down by the gastric juices. Eventually, after about four hours, it forms a semi-solid mass which passes into the small intestine. The small intestine is lined with millions of tiny, finger-like projections called villi which are especially designed to assimilate nutrients into the blood and the lymph system. Once the nutrients are removed, the remaining material, which cannot be used, passes through the large intestine and is eliminated by the body. The complete cycle lasts about 12 hours.

Chew Food Thoroughly

Chewing is an essential part of the digestive process. It is very important to chew foods thoroughly so that they can be broken down more easily in the stomach. The longer you chew, the more the food is mixed with saliva, which also facilitates digestion.

Digestive Upsets

The digestive process is easily upset. The digestive juices and the muscle contractions in the digestive tract are affected by environmental stimuli. If food is presented in an attractive fashion, if the dining room is filled with delicious aromas, if the atmosphere is relaxed and the conversation flows, then the process of digestion is likely to take place with no problems. In the same way, outside circumstances can impede the production of the digestive juices. Psychological trauma, stress, fright or anger can all result in poor digestion. Harmonious mealtimes therefore have a direct bearing on the nutritional benefits of the food you eat.

Water and Fiber: Essential Allies

Water is essential to all life and plays a major role in the way our bodies and our digestive systems work. It helps to dissolve nutrients and to transport them to the cells that need them. It also facilitates the elimination of waste products. So be sure to drink eight large glasses of water each day. The kidneys will easily get rid of extra water.

Food fiber was scorned for many years and was systematically removed in many refining processes that claimed to make food pure. Today, however, it is frequently looked upon as a miracle substance. Food fiber, although not assimilated by the body, has only quite recently been known to be very important to the body for its function of facilitating the movement of waste products through the intestine. It is found in fruits and vegetables but even more so in whole grain cereals, particularly in bran. Cereal fiber has the added advantage of being able to absorb large quantities of water; this quality helps to soften the waste material formed, making it easy to pass.

Drinking large quantities of water and eating foods that are rich in fiber each day will make an important contribution to your health.

MICROTIPS

The Use of Dry Legumes in Different Cooking Traditions

The most well-known dishes in Canada that make use of dry legumes are pork and beans and pea soup. However, legumes have been a part of cooking traditions for many centuries and are extensively used throughout the world. France has cassoulet, Mexico has chili con carne, Algeria has lentil soup, Libya has couscous with chick peas and so on.

Legumes are easy to prepare but are frequently rejected as being difficult to digest and liable to cause flatulence. However, if you cook them thoroughly and chew them well you can avoid these problems. It is also a good idea to discard the water used to soak them and to cook them in fresh water. Unlike vegetables, legumes should be cooked so that they are easy to mash with a fork.

Microwave Cooking: Healthy Cooking

Microwave cooking has several advantages over traditional methods of cooking. These advantages can be very beneficial to you if you decide to work hard at ensuring that your diet is healthy and balanced. You can change your eating habits without completely revolutionizing your lifestyle.

Less Heat, More Vitamins

Microwave cooking is the perfect method for those who want to cook in a hurry but who do not want to destroy fragile vitamins by overexposure to high temperatures.

As you know, heating food in the microwave takes just a few seconds and a piece of meat can be cooked in a matter of minutes.

Because the actual cooking time is shorter, microwaving preserves vitamins that are easily destroyed by heat, such as Vitamin B_1. The taste, texture and color of food are preserved by this cooking method as well.

Less Water, More Vitamins

Microwave cooking also requires very little water because it makes use of the water content of the food being cooked. You can cook most vegetables, such as mushrooms, spinach and jacket potatoes, simply by putting them on a piece of paper towel or in a dish and microwaving them for a few minutes. Only vegetables that have a low water content, such as carrots and rutabagas, need additional water in the cooking dish. As a result, microwave cooking helps preserve the vitamins that are soluble in water.

Low-Fat Cooking: A Dieter's Dream

Microwave cooking requires very little fat. As heat is generated by the action of the food molecules bouncing off each other and is not transferred to the food from the dish itself, the food will not stick. Washing up is also easier and your food is healthier.

The Nutritional Value of Some Common Foods

Milk and Dairy Products				
Food	Quantity	Calories	Protein (g)	Calcium (mg)
Camembert cheese	45 g (1-1/2 oz)	135	9	175
Cheddar cheese	45 g (1-1/2 oz)	181	11	324
Cottage cheese (2%)	250 mL (1 cup)	213	33	165
Whole milk	250 mL (1 cup)	160	8	288
2% milk	250 mL (1 cup)	123	8	283
Chocolate milk	250 mL (1 cup)	230	8	280
Milk shake	250 mL (1 cup)	233	12	393
Mozzarella cheese	45 g (1-1/2 oz)	126	9	233
Plain yoghurt	125 mL (1/2 cup)	85	6	203

The Nutritional Value of Some Common Foods

Fruits and Vegetables

Food	Quantity	Calories	Vitamin A (I.U.)	Vitamin C (mg)
Broccoli, cooked	250 mL (1 cup)	42	3715	148
Carrot, raw	1	20	5500	4
Carrot, cooked	250 mL (1 cup)	47	15220	9
Celery, raw	1 stick	5	100	4
Apple (juice)	250 mL (1 cup)	130	—	93
Blueberries	250 mL (1 cup)	85	140	20
Orange (juice)	250 mL (1 cup)	116	500	108
Strawberries	250 mL (1 cup)	55	90	88

Meat, Fish, Poultry and Alternates

Food	Quantity	Calories	Protein (g)	Iron (mg)
Beef liver, fried	3 slices	206	24	15.0
Cashew nuts, roasted	125 mL (1/2 cup)	415	13	2.5
Chicken, roasted	4 slices	122	21	0.5
Egg, boiled	1	79	6	0.8
Haddock, cooked	1 fillet	140	16	1.0
Lamb, leg	2 slices	251	23	5.2
Navy beans, cooked	250 mL (1 cup)	205	15	5.1
Pork sausage	1	55	3	0.2
Steak, grilled	1 slice	318	22	3.0
Sunflower seeds	125 mL (1/2 cup)	325	15	5.2
Tuna, canned	125 mL (1/2 cup)	177	26	1.6

Bread and Cereals

Food	Quantity	Calories	Protein (g)	Calcium (mg)
Bran muffin	1	120	3	57
Bread, enriched white	1 slice	82	2	18
Bread, 100% whole wheat	1 slice	70	3	30
Cheese crackers	4	50	1	40
Granola	125 mL (1/2 cup)	288	6	34
Pancake, plain	1	60	2	58
Porridge, oats	125 mL (1/2 cup)	69	3	21
Rice, polished white	250 mL (1 cup)	195	4	35

Feeling Peckish?
Or Ravenous? Think Soup!

Soup is so easy to prepare in the microwave oven that you might think this method of cooking was developed especially to deal with it. You can make it, defrost it or heat it in next to no time. For this reason, we have dedicated a special section in each volume of *Health Cookery* to the preparation of soups.

Any of the recipes on the following pages could be served as a starter to a special meal or on their own as a light lunch. Small helpings of cream of rutabaga or carrot soup, for example, could be served to begin a full-course meal. The more robust soups, such as minestrone soup and beef soup, could be served with sandwiches, crackers and cheese or a salad as a main meal to satisfy the heartiest appetites.

Soups are generally rich in vitamins because they usually contain numerous vegetables. Also, soups are extremely simple to make; no special skills and no exotic, hard-to-find ingredients are needed to create a great soup.

The secret of a good soup lies in the stock used in its preparation. Most recipes call for chicken stock but a good vegetable stock can certainly be substituted. In any case, you probably have chicken or beef stock cubes in your cupboard, but you should be aware that stock cubes contain a great deal of salt.

Get in the habit of boiling up poultry carcasses or meat bones to make stock. It can be kept in the freezer, to be used when you want to make a really good soup. Do the same with vegetable water; it is rich in vitamins and so it is worth allowing it to cool and then freezing it in an airtight container. Add to the container whenever you have more vegetable water. However, do not use the water in which cabbage has been cooked—it has too strong a flavor and can overpower your vegetable stock.

Soups are suited to splendid occasions and are great for meals in a hurry. So, whether you are an experienced cook or a beginner, you can try these soup recipes without any hesitation because they are amazingly simple to make— and are bound to be a great success.

Cucumber and Tomato Soup

Level of Difficulty	🍴
Preparation Time	20 min*
Cost per Serving	$
Number of Servings	8
Nutritional Value	46 calories 8.1 g carbohydrate 22.4 mg Vitamin C
Food Exchanges	2 vegetable exchanges
Cooking Time	3 min
Standing Time	None
Power Level	100%
Write Your Cooking Time Here	

* This soup should be refrigerated for 1 hour before serving.

Ingredients
4 cucumbers
2 tomatoes
250 mL (1 cup) chicken stock
1 small onion, chopped
1 clove garlic, chopped
10 mL (2 teaspoons) basil
250 mL (1 cup) 2% milk
salt and pepper to taste
15 mL (1 tablespoon) parsley

Method
— Peel, seed and chop the cucumbers; set aside.
— Peel and chop the tomatoes; set aside.
— Heat the chicken stock at 100% for 3 minutes.
— Pour the chicken stock into a blender and add the cucumbers, tomatoes and all the other ingredients except the parsley.
— Blend for a few seconds until smooth.
— Refrigerate for 1 hour.
— Season to taste and garnish with parsley before serving cold.

This recipe will add a novel
touch to any menu, particularly
summer menus. Assemble all
the ingredients before you begin
to cook.

Peel, seed and chop the
cucumbers; peel the tomatoes
and chop them.

Pour the hot chicken stock into
a blender and add the
cucumbers, tomatoes and all
the other ingredients except the
parsley.

Beef Soup

Level of Difficulty	🍴
Preparation Time	30 min
Cost per Serving	$
Number of Servings	8
Nutritional Value	133 calories 13.8 g protein 2.3 mg iron
Food Exchanges	2 oz meat 1 vegetable exchange
Cooking Time	41 min
Standing Time	5 min
Power Level	100%
Write Your Cooking Time Here	✏️🍎

Ingredients
450 g (1 lb) lean ground beef
1 clove garlic, chopped
50 mL (1/4 cup) celery, thinly sliced
50 mL (1/4 cup) onion, chopped
1 540 mL (19 oz) can tomatoes, chopped
1 L (4 cups) beef stock
125 mL (1/2 cup) cauliflower, chopped
125 mL (1/2 cup) broccoli, chopped
125 mL (1/2 cup) carrots, grated
5 mL (1 teaspoon) thyme
salt and pepper to taste

Method
— Put the ground beef and garlic in a deep dish; cook at 100% for 4 to 6 minutes, stirring twice with a fork during the cooking time to break up the meat, and set aside.
— Put the celery, onion and tomatoes in a dish; cover and cook at 100% for 4 to 5 minutes, stirring once during the cooking time.
— Add the cooked vegetables and the remaining ingredients to the meat; mix well and season to taste.
— Cover the dish and cook at 100% for 20 to 30 minutes, stirring several times.
— Allow to stand for 5 minutes.

26

Crab Soup

Level of Difficulty	🍴
Preparation Time	20 min
Cost per Serving	$ $
Number of Servings	8
Nutritional Value	102 calories 8.4 g protein 1.2 mg Vitamin C
Food Exchanges	1 oz meat 1 vegetable exchange
Cooking Time	22 min
Standing Time	None
Power Level	100%
Write Your Cooking Time Here	

Ingredients
1 213 mL (7-1/2 oz) can crabmeat
3 leeks, white parts only, sliced
4 potatoes, peeled and sliced
750 mL (3 cups) chicken stock
500 mL (2 cups) 2% milk
salt and pepper to taste
watercress to garnish

Method
— Put the leeks and potatoes in a deep dish with 125 mL (1/2 cup) of the chicken stock.
— Cover and cook at 100% for 4 to 6 minutes, stirring once during the cooking time.
— Add the remaining stock; cover and cook at 100% for 10 minutes, stirring once during the cooking time.
— Pour the mixture into a blender, add the milk and blend for a few seconds until smooth.
— Add the crabmeat.
— Season to taste and pour the mixture into a deep dish.
— Heat at 100% for 4 to 6 minutes, but do not allow the soup to boil.
— Garnish with watercress before serving.

This delicious soup will satisfy even the most demanding palate. Here are the ingredients to be assembled before you begin to cook.

Cook the leeks and potatoes in 125 mL (1/2 cup) of the chicken stock. Then add the remaining stock and cook for 10 minutes longer.

Put the cooked ingredients into a blender, add the milk and blend until smooth.

Cream of Rutabaga Soup

Level of Difficulty	🍴🍽
Preparation Time	20 min
Cost per Serving	**$**
Number of Servings	4
Nutritional Value	48 calories 3.3 g protein 10.6 mg Vitamin C
Food Exchanges	2 vegetable exchanges
Cooking Time	19 min
Standing Time	None
Power Level	100%
Write Your Cooking Time Here	✏️🍎

Ingredients
250 mL (1 cup) rutabaga, diced
125 mL (1/2 cup) onion, chopped
125 mL (1/2 cup) celery, chopped
375 mL (1-1/2 cups) chicken stock
5 mL (1 teaspoon) fine herbs
250 mL (1 cup) 2% milk
salt and pepper to taste
parsley, chopped

Method
— Put the rutabaga, onion, celery and 125 mL (1/2 cup) of the chicken stock in a deep dish.
— Cover and cook at 100% for 7 to 9 minutes, stirring once during the cooking time.
— Add the remaining stock and continue to cook at 100% for 5 minutes, stirring once during the cooking time.
— Pour the cooked ingredients into a blender, add the fine herbs and season to taste.
— Purée for a few seconds until smooth and add the milk.
— Pour the soup into the deep dish and heat at 100% for 4 to 5 minutes, stirring once during the cooking time. Do not allow the soup to boil.
— Garnish with parsley before serving.

First assemble the ingredients for this easy-to-make soup, one that is suitable for any occasion.

Transfer the cooked ingredients to a blender and add the fine herbs. Purée for a few seconds until smooth and add the milk.

MICROTIPS

Enjoy Stuffed Squash Throughout the Year

To prepare stuffed squash, select winter squash that is fully ripe but still small. Winter squash differs from summer squash in that it has harder, more fibrous flesh, a tougher skin and hard seeds that are not edible. The seeds must therefore be removed, creating a pocket that can be filled.

31

Carrot Soup

Level of Difficulty	🍴
Preparation Time	20 min
Cost per Serving	**$**
Number of Servings	8
Nutritional Value	44 calories 5.8 g carbohydrate 2840 I.U. Vitamin A
Food Exchanges	2 vegetable exchanges
Cooking Time	26 min
Standing Time	None
Power Level	100%
Write Your Cooking Time Here	

Ingredients
625 mL (2-1/2 cups) carrots, thinly sliced
1 onion, chopped
1 clove garlic, thinly sliced
1.25 L (5 cups) chicken stock
50 mL (1/4 cup) white rice, cooked
salt and pepper to taste
15 mL (1 tablespoon) butter
parsley, chopped

Method
— Put the carrots, onion, garlic and 125 mL (1/2 cup) of the stock in a deep dish.
— Cover and cook at 100% for 5 to 8 minutes, stirring once.
— Add the remaining stock and the cooked rice.
— Cover and continue to cook at 100% for 10 to 12 minutes, stirring once.
— Pour the cooked ingredients into a blender and purée for a few seconds until smooth.
— Season to taste and pour the soup back into the deep dish.
— Heat at 100% for 4 to 6 minutes, stirring once.
— Add the butter and parsley; stir well before serving.

Minestrone Soup

Level of Difficulty	
Preparation Time	20 min
Cost per Serving	**$**
Number of Servings	8
Nutritional Value	107 calories 17.9 g carbohydrate 2562 I.U. Vitamin A
Food Exchanges	3 vegetable exchanges 1/2 bread exchange
Cooking Time	28 min
Standing Time	None
Power Level	100%
Write Your Cooking Time Here	

Ingredients
2 cloves garlic, chopped
1 onion, thinly sliced
2 carrots, thinly sliced
1 potato, diced
1.5 L (6 cups) chicken stock
500 mL (2 cups) tomatoes, peeled, drained and chopped
2 small zucchini, thinly sliced
2 mL (1/2 teaspoon) basil
1 bay leaf
salt and pepper to taste
250 mL (1 cup) chick peas, cooked
50 mL (1/4 cup) parsley, chopped

Method
— Put the garlic, onion, carrots, potato and 125 mL (1/2 cup) of the stock in a deep dish.
— Cover and cook at 100% for 5 to 6 minutes, stirring once during the cooking time.
— Add the tomatoes, zucchini, basil, bay leaf and the remaining stock; season to taste.
— Cook at 100% for 15 minutes, stirring once during the cooking time.
— Add the chick peas.
— Continue to cook at 100% for 5 to 7 minutes, stirring once during the cooking time.
— Remove the bay leaf, add the parsley and mix well.
— Check the seasoning and adjust to taste before serving.

You can combine all these ingredients to make a highly nutritious soup in less than an hour.

Add the chick peas before the final cooking period.

Once the soup is cooked, remove the bay leaf and add the parsley.

Cream of Leek and Broccoli Soup

Level of Difficulty	
Preparation Time	15 min
Cost per Serving	**$**
Number of Servings	6
Nutritional Value	86.4 calories 7.3 g carbohydrate 205 mg calcium
Food Exchanges	1 vegetable exchange 1/2 milk exchange
Cooking Time	24 min
Standing Time	None
Power Level	100%
Write Your Cooking Time Here	

Ingredients
2 leeks, cut into pieces
1 head of broccoli, chopped
75 mL (1/3 cup) chicken stock
875 mL (3-1/2 cups) 2% milk
1 bay leaf
salt and pepper to taste
chives, chopped

Method
— Put the leeks, broccoli and stock in a deep dish.
— Cover and cook at 100% for 6 to 9 minutes, stirring once during the cooking time.
— Add the milk, the bay leaf and season to taste.
— Continue to cook at 100% for 10 minutes, stirring once during the cooking time.
— Remove the bay leaf, pour the ingredients into a blender and purée.
— Pour the soup back into the deep dish and heat at 100% for 4 to 5 minutes, stirring once during the cooking time.
— Garnish with chives before serving.

Begin by assembling these few ingredients and you will be able to make this cream of leek and broccoli soup in next to no time.

Add the milk and the bay leaf before the second stage of cooking.

MICROTIPS

Dry Legumes

Dry legumes freeze very well. In order to make full use of the protein in them, serve them with a cereal or with an animal protein such as meat or a dairy product.

Starters

Starters allow the cook to be somewhat creative. At the same time, they set the tone for the remainder of the meal. It is therefore important to have them hit the right note and, because you are concerned about healthy eating, to prepare them with nutritious ingredients that will complement those in the other foods you plan to serve at the same meal. Within these guidelines, it is perfectly acceptable to be original and innovative; you will find many starter recipes in this volume that fit into this category.

Starters are often prepared in tiny, bite-size portions and arranged on a serving platter so that the guests may select exactly what they want. They can be passed around the living room on trays or left on the coffee table for the guests to help themselves while the cook puts the final touches on the meal.

If you want more time to chat with guests before dinner, serve finger foods as a starter. Cubes of cheese may sound mundane but you will find more variety than the standard cheddar at the cheese counter—you can choose wonderful cheeses from all over the world, including Gorgonzola, Havarti, triple crème, chèvre and so on, which are bound to win compliments.

Remember, though, that there is no reason to limit yourself to cold dishes. With the microwave oven it is easy to make food in advance and reheat it just prior to serving; try mini-meatballs, tiny wedges of pizza, mini-sausages and stuffed mushroom caps.

As this volume focuses on cooking for health, the starter recipes offered include a large number of vegetables. As shown in the food charts, many recipes contain the equivalent of two or three servings of vegetables. These starters therefore make it easy for you to follow the Canadian Food Guide recommendation that four or five servings of vegetables be included in your daily diet. The Ratatouille, Broccoli Terrine and Zucchini Provençale provide new and interesting ways to include extra vegetables in your meal.

If you ever find yourself short of inspiration about what to serve as a starter, remember that you can always serve a small helping of a main dish.

Once you have accumulated a good selection of starter recipes, you will find that you are quickly and easily able to transform ordinary meals into memorable occasions.

Ratatouille

Level of Difficulty	🍴
Preparation Time	30 min
Cost per Serving	$
Number of Servings	10
Nutritional Value	91 calories 10.6 g carbohydrate 50 mg Vitamin C
Food Exchanges	2 vegetable exchanges 1 fat exchange
Cooking Time	13 min
Standing Time	4 min
Power Level	100%
Write Your Cooking Time Here	

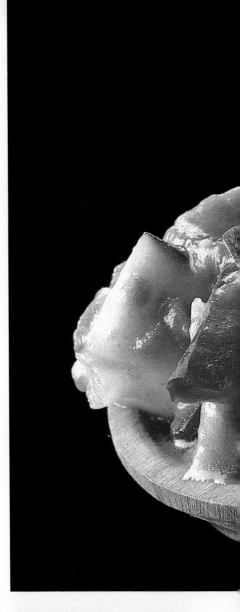

Ingredients
2 cloves garlic, finely chopped
1 onion, chopped
50 mL (1/4 cup) butter
50 mL (1/4 cup) flour
1 L (4 cups) tomatoes, peeled and chopped, with their liquid
2 zucchini, unpeeled and cut into cubes
1 eggplant, unpeeled and diced
2 red peppers, cut into strips
salt and pepper to taste

Method
— Put the garlic, onion and butter into a deep dish.
— Cover and cook at 100% for 3 to 4 minutes.
— Add the flour and mix well.
— Add the tomatoes and their liquid and mix.
— Add the zucchini, eggplant and red peppers; mix well and season to taste.
— Cover and cook at 100% for 7 to 9 minutes, stirring once during the cooking time.
— Allow to stand for 4 minutes.

This delicious ratatouille can be served hot or cold. Here are the ingredients that should be assembled before you begin to prepare it.

Add the tomatoes, including their liquid, to the garlic, onion, butter and flour.

Stir the vegetable once during the final cooking period to ensure that they cook evenly.

MICROTIPS

About Tomatoes

Out of season, you will find that canned tomatoes are much cheaper than fresh ones. Also, because tomatoes are canned shortly after they are picked, they generally contain more vitamins than out-of-season tomatoes, which have been transported a great distance.

Broccoli Terrine

Level of Difficulty	🍴🍴 🍴🍴
Preparation Time	20 min
Cost per Serving	**$**
Number of Servings	4
Nutritional Value	329 calories 24.4 g carbohydrate 588 mg calcium
Food Exchanges	3 oz meat 1 vegetable exchange 1/4 milk exchange
Cooking Time	11 min
Standing Time	5 min
Power Level	100%, 70%
Write Your Cooking Time Here	

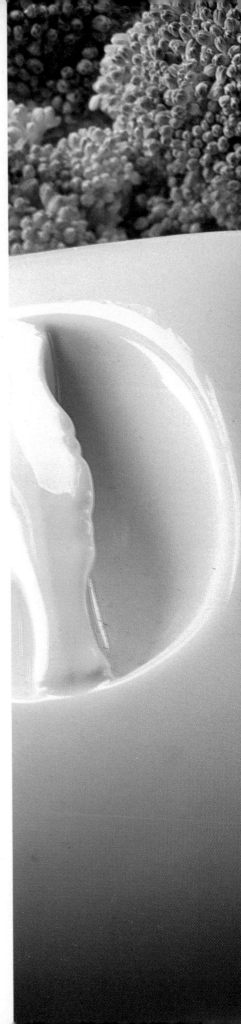

Ingredients
1 head of broccoli, cooked, drained and chopped
30 mL (2 tablespoons) butter
30 mL (2 tablespoons) flour
250 mL (1 cup) 2% milk
250 g (9 oz) mozzarella cheese, grated
salt and pepper to taste
1 onion, finely chopped
2 egg whites
2 egg yolks
paprika to garnish

Method
— Put the butter into a dish and heat at 100% for 30 seconds to melt it.
— Add the flour and mix well.
— Add the milk and cook at 100% for 3 to 4 minutes, stirring vigorously twice during the cooking time.
— Add the mozzarella cheese, stirring constantly until it melts.
— Season to taste.
— Add the onion and the cooked broccoli and set aside.
— Beat the egg whites until stiff.
— Beat the egg yolks and add them to the cheese sauce and broccoli.
— Use a spatula to fold the egg whites into the mixture.
— Grease a 22.5 cm (9 inch) by 12 cm (5 inch) loaf pan.

⇒

Broccoli Terrine

This recipe for broccoli terrine provides you with a wonderful opportunity to serve a highly nutritious vegetable in an original way. Here are the ingredients you will need.

Add the milk to the butter and flour and cook at 100% for 3 to 4 minutes, stirring vigorously twice during the cooking time.

Add the mozzarella cheese, stirring constantly so that it melts.

Add the onion and cooked broccoli and set the mixture aside.

Use a spatula to fold the beaten egg whites into the mixture.

Place the loaf pan on a rack in the oven, cook at 70% for 3 minutes and give it a half-turn. Continue to cook for 3 to 4 minutes longer.

— Pour the mixture into the loaf pan.
— Sprinkle with paprika.
— Place the pan on a rack in the oven and cook at 70% for 3 minutes.
— Give the pan a half-turn and continue to cook for 3 to 4 minutes.
— Allow to stand for 5 minutes before serving.

Liver Loaf

Ingredients

450 g (1 lb) beef liver
500 mL (2 cups) water
125 mL (1/2 cup, or
approximately 2 slices) dry
bread, crusts removed
1 onion, chopped
1 carrot, grated
225 g (1/2 lb) lean ground
beef
2 eggs, beaten
1 mL (1/4 teaspoon) allspice
1 mL (1/4 teaspoon) thyme
1 mL (1/4 teaspoon) basil
salt and pepper to taste
125 mL (1/2 cup) tomato
juice

Method

— Pour the water into a dish
and bring to a boil by
heating at 100% for 7 to 9
minutes.
— Put the liver into a bowl
and pour the water on
top; allow to cool.
— Drain the liver and chop
coarsely.
— Place the liver, bread and
onion in a bowl; mix well
and put through a meat
grinder.
— Add the carrot, ground
beef, eggs and seasonings
to the mixture.
— Mix well until smooth and
add the tomato juice.
— Place the mixture in a
greased loaf pan.
— Put the pan on a rack in
the oven and cook at
100% for 5 minutes.
— Give the pan a half-turn
and reduce the power level
to 50%.
— Continue to cook for 25 to
30 minutes, giving the
dish a half-turn halfway
through the cooking time.
— Allow to stand for 10
minutes before serving,
with an accompanying
tomato sauce if desired.

Navy Beans with Pineapple

Level of Difficulty	🍴
Preparation Time	15 min*
Cost per Serving	**$**
Number of Servings	6
Nutritional Value	254 calories 13.1 g protein 44 g carbohydrate
Food Exchanges	3 oz meat 1 vegetable exchange
Cooking Time	3 h 10 min
Standing Time	None
Power Level	100%, 50%
Write Your Cooking Time Here	

* The beans should be left to soak in water for 12 hours before cooking.

Ingredients
450 g (1 lb) navy beans
1 onion, chopped
30 mL (2 tablespoons) brown sugar
175 mL (3/4 cup) tomato sauce
5 mL (1 teaspoon) mustard powder
10 mL (2 teaspoons) vinegar
5 mL (1 teaspoon) HP sauce
250 mL (1 cup) crushed pineapple

Method
— Put the beans into a dish and cover with cold water.
— Allow to soak for 12 hours.
— Drain the beans and add fresh water; cover and cook at 100% for 40 minutes, stirring once during the cooking time.
— Drain the beans and reserve the water; add all the other ingredients to the beans and mix well.
— Add just enough of the reserved bean water to cover the ingredients; reserve the remainder of the water to add to the beans as required during the cooking.
— Cover and cook at 100% for 30 minutes.
— Reduce the power level to 50% and cook for 1 to 2 hours, or until the beans are done to your liking, stirring every 30 minutes and checking frequently for the need to add more water.

An unusual way of preparing beans, this dish will surprise your guests. Here are the ingredients that you should assemble.

Soak the beans, drain and cook them in fresh water. Drain them, reserving the water, and mix the beans with the remaining ingredients.

Stir the beans every 30 minutes during the cooking and check frequently to ensure that they are always just covered with water.

Broccoli with Mushrooms

Level of Difficulty	🍴
Preparation Time	15 min
Cost per Serving	$
Number of Servings	4
Nutritional Value	44 calories 4.9 g carbohydrate 688 mg Vitamin C
Food Exchanges	2 vegetable exchanges
Cooking Time	9 min
Standing Time	None
Power Level	100%
Write Your Cooking Time Here	

Ingredients
500 mL (2 cups) broccoli flowerets
50 mL (1/4 cup) water
10 mL (2 teaspoons) butter
4 large mushrooms, sliced
2 green onions, chopped
5 mL (1 teaspoon) flour
30 mL (2 tablespoons) water
5 mL (1 teaspoon) soy sauce

Method
— Put the broccoli in a dish and add the 50 mL (1/4 cup) water; cover and cook at 100% for 4 to 5 minutes, stirring once during the cooking time.
— Drain the broccoli and set aside.
— Put the butter, mushrooms and green onions in a dish; cover and cook at 100% for 2 to 3 minutes, stirring once during the cooking time. Set aside.
— In a small bowl, blend the flour with the 30 mL (2 tablespoons) water and the soy sauce and stir until smooth.
— Add to the mushrooms and green onions.
— Cook at 100% for 1 minute, or until the sauce thickens slightly, stirring once during the cooking time.
— Arrange the broccoli flowerets in a serving dish, add the sauce, stir gently and reheat before serving.

48

Your guests are bound to enjoy this delicious vegetable dish. Here are the ingredients that should be assembled to prepare it.

Begin by cooking the broccoli in a covered dish with 50 mL (1/4 cup) water.

Blend the flour with the water and the soy sauce and add to the mushrooms and green onions. Cook as directed.

49

Stuffed Mushroom Caps

Level of Difficulty	🍴
Preparation Time	15 min
Cost per Serving	**$**
Number of Servings	4
Nutritional Value	59 calories 5.1 g carbohydrate 1110.4 mg potassium
Food Exchanges	2 vegetable exchanges
Cooking Time	7 min
Standing Time	None
Power Level	100%
Write Your Cooking Time Here	

Ingredients
12 large mushrooms
10 mL (2 teaspoons) butter
125 mL (1/2 cup) celery,
finely chopped
50 mL (1/4 cup) green onion,
finely chopped
1 clove garlic, crushed
30 mL (2 tablespoons)
Parmesan cheese, grated
15 mL (1 tablespoon)
breadcrumbs
salt and pepper to taste
15 mL (1 tablespoon) parsley,
chopped

Method
— Wash and dry the
mushrooms.
— Cut off the mushroom
stalks and chop finely;
reserve the caps.
— Combine the chopped
mushroom stalks, butter,
celery, green onion,
garlic, Parmesan cheese
and breadcrumbs in a
dish; mix well and season
to taste.
— Cook at 100% for 3 to 4
minutes, stirring once
during the cooking time.
— Stuff the mushroom caps
with this mixture and
arrange them in a circle on
a large plate.
— Heat at 100% for 2 to 3
minutes, giving the dish a
half-turn halfway through
the cooking time.
— Garnish with chopped
parsley and serve.

⟹

Stuffed Mushroom Caps

Stuffed mushrooms, always popular, can be served as a starter or as an accompanying vegetable. Assemble these ingredients before you begin to cook.

Wash the mushrooms and dry them carefully with paper towel.

Use a knife to cut the stalks off the mushrooms.

Chop the mushroom stalks finely.

Combine the ingredients for the stuffing and stir during the cooking time to ensure that it cooks evenly.

Arrange the mushroom caps in a circle on a large plate to heat them through.

MICROTIPS

Homemade Breadcrumbs

You can buy ready-made breadcrumbs in any food store, but it is both easy and economical to make your own in the blender.

Put leftover stale bread, broken crackers, stale potato chips and even crumbs of unsweetened cereal into a large container and leave them to dry out. When you have a large enough quantity, put the mixture into the blender and blend at high speed for a couple of minutes. If you want crumbs with an even texture, cut the bread into large cubes before leaving it to dry out.

Zucchini Provençale

Ingredients

2 zucchini, thinly sliced
15 mL (1 tablespoon) oil
125 mL (1/2 cup) onion, finely chopped
1 clove garlic, chopped
175 mL (3/4 cup) tomatoes, peeled, chopped and drained
2 mL (1/2 teaspoon) basil
salt and pepper to taste
50 mL (1/4 cup) black olives, pitted and cut in half
50 mL (1/4 cup) Parmesan cheese, grated

Method

— Combine the oil, onion and garlic in a large dish; cover and cook at 100% for 2 minutes, stirring once.
— Add the tomatoes, zucchini and basil and season to taste.
— Cover and cook at 100% for 7 to 9 minutes, stirring once.
— Add the olives and mix well; cover and allow to stand for 5 minutes.
— Garnish with the Parmesan cheese.

Level of Difficulty	🍴
Preparation Time	15 min
Cost per Serving	$
Number of Servings	6
Nutritional Value	64 calories 2.8 g protein 9.4 mg Vitamin C
Food Exchanges	3 vegetable exchanges
Cooking Time	11 min
Standing Time	5 min
Power Level	100%
Write Your Cooking Time Here	

Main Dishes

Main dishes that are worthy of the name should provide a generous serving of protein, which is essential to the health of body tissue. As a result, most main dishes include meat, poultry, fish, seafood or alternates.

The warnings about the amount of cholesterol found in red meat have been so numerous that it has, to some extent, lost its popularity. However, there is no harm in serving your family red meat from time to time. Microwave cooking can help set your mind at rest about red meat because it requires little extra fat. Also, the meat is frequently cooked on a rack, allowing nearly all of its fat content to drain. It should be remembered that beef, veal and lamb are rich in protein and these meats, when ground, can be served in countless ways: in casseroles, as meatballs, in hash and as meat loaves—all of which are great for satisfying the heartiest of appetites.

Poultry, readily taking on the subtle flavor of aromatics, is always a main dish favorite. Whether you are serving plain chicken with steamed rice or a sophisticated dish of duck with orange sauce, the cooking time must be carefully watched to ensure that the flesh remains tender and juicy. Poultry has the same nutritional value whether you buy it fresh or frozen, whole or cut into serving pieces. One advantage in buying whole, fresh birds, however, is that the giblets (wings, neck, heart, liver, gizzard), which can be used to make a delicious stock, come with them. In the past few years, grain-fed chicken has been available to people who are particularly health conscious. Grain-fed chickens are raised in controlled conditions and fed grain rather than prepared feed, and they are larger than ordinary chickens. If you plan to serve one, remember to adjust the quantities of the other ingredients used and the number of servings expected accordingly.

Fish has been standard Friday fare for many years and until recently was somewhat looked down upon. Today, however, it is gaining in popularity. Once, the fish counter was the least populated and least attractive area in the frozen food section; now, many stores have enormous fish counters and sell quantities of both fish and seafood. You will find fillets of sole, hake, haddock, cod, salmon steaks and whole rainbow trout alongside pink and gray shrimps, clams, scallops and lobsters. If your only experience with fish is with frozen fish, try eating it fresh —there is a world of difference in the taste.

Legumes also contain protein. However, the incomplete protein in them must be combined with other protein —either complete or incomplete—in order to have the same nutritional value as meat. It is for this reason that, in Mexican traditions, chili con carne (a dish that includes kidney beans) is served with corn bread (a cereal). For the same reason, most lentil dishes are served with rice. In days gone by, the traditional beans and bacon were served with hefty slices of whole wheat bread; popular common sense must have had some insight into healthy eating!

The recipes for main dishes given on the following pages are bound to please everyone and will surely make you and your family enthusiastic about healthy cooking.

Chicken with White Wine

Level of Difficulty	 (utensils icon)
Preparation Time	30 min
Cost per Serving	$ $
Number of Servings	4
Nutritional Value	323 calories 39.9 g protein 2.8 mg iron
Food Exchanges	3-1/2 oz meat 2 vegetable exchanges 1 fat exchange
Cooking Time	28 min
Standing Time	5 min
Power Level	100%, 70%
Write Your Cooking Time Here	

Ingredients

1 chicken, 1.3 kg (3 lb), cut into serving pieces
30 mL (2 tablespoons) oil
250 mL (1 cup) onion, thinly sliced
250 mL (1 cup) mushrooms, thinly sliced
125 mL (1/2 cup) carrots, grated
2 sticks celery, diced
1 clove garlic, crushed
250 mL (1 cup) white wine
30 mL (2 tablespoons) parsley, chopped
2 mL (1/2 teaspoon) thyme
1 bay leaf

Method

— Remove the skin from the chicken pieces.
— Preheat a browning dish at 100% for 7 minutes and add the oil.
— Heat at 100% for 30 seconds and sear the chicken pieces.
— Remove the chicken pieces and set aside.
— Heat the browning dish again, at 100% for 4 minutes.
— Sauté the onion, mushrooms, carrots, celery and garlic.
— Cover and cook at 100% for 3 minutes, stirring once during the cooking time.
— Add the chicken pieces and the remaining ingredients.
— Cover again and reduce the power level to 70%.
— Cook for 20 to 25 minutes, rearranging the chicken pieces halfway through the cooking time.
— Allow to stand for 5 minutes before serving.

This recipe is always popular and calls for these simple, everyday ingredients.

Sear the chicken pieces in the oil in the preheated browning dish.

Heat the browning dish a second time for 4 minutes and sauté the vegetables.

Chicken with Yoghurt

Level of Difficulty	🍴🔪
Preparation Time	20 min
Cost per Serving	**$**
Number of Servings	6
Nutritional Value	208 calories 29.3 g protein 57.4 g carbohydrate
Food Exchanges	3 oz meat 1 vegetable exchange 1/2 fat exchange
Cooking Time	22 min
Standing Time	None
Power Level	100%, 70%
Write Your Cooking Time Here	

Ingredients
3 whole chicken breasts,
boned, skinned and cut in half
125 mL (1/2 cup) plain
yoghurt
15 mL (1 tablespoon) flour
30 mL (2 tablespoons) butter
115 g (4 oz) mushrooms, cut
in half
2 onions, chopped
125 mL (1/2 cup) water
5 mL (1 teaspoon) tarragon
15 mL (1 tablespoon) parsley,
chopped
salt and pepper to taste

Method

— Lightly dredge the chicken breast halves with the flour.

— Preheat a browning dish at 100% for 7 minutes and add the butter.

— Heat at 100% for 30 seconds and sear the chicken by turning it in the butter until it is completely golden.

— Add the mushrooms and onions and cover.

— Reduce the power level to 70% and cook for 15 to 20 minutes, or until the chicken is done.

— Remove the chicken and vegetables and set aside.

— Pour the water into the browning dish and heat at 100% for 1 minute.

— Deglaze the pan and add the yoghurt, tarragon and parsley; season to taste.

— Cook at 100% for 1 minute, stirring once during the cooking time.

— Add the vegetables and mix them with the yoghurt.

— Pour the yoghurt sauce over the chicken before serving.

MICROTIPS

Meat Needs Company
Always serve meat dishes accompanied by a vegetable. When fresh vegetables are out of season buy frozen ones. They will be less expensive than fresh and are very nutritious.

To Get Enough Iron

Serve a piece of fruit or a vegetable with a high Vitamin C content, such as pineapple, cantaloupe, strawberries or broccoli, when legumes are on the menu; the combination enables the body to make the most of the iron in the legumes.

Chicken with Yoghurt

It is easy to make this recipe successfully. Begin by assembling these ingredients.

Lightly dredge the chicken with the flour and then sear it in the butter in the preheated browning dish.

Remove the chicken and cooked vegetables and deglaze the pan with the water to make the sauce.

Feel Better and Enjoy Life More

Make a point of varying your choice of food and taking the trouble to present it attractively. These two guidelines alone will make it easier to stick to a healthy diet.

For Your Health . . .

No single food contains all the nutrients our bodies need to stay healthy. Some nutrients may be completely missing in certain foods or present only in minute amounts.

For example, our bodies need only tiny amounts of such trace elements as copper, magnesium and nickel. However, these elements are not found in equal quantities in all foods. Complex calculations would have to be made to work out if the potatoes you ate last night provided you with a sufficient number of trace elements. So what can you do to avoid the bother of becoming an amateur dietitian? The answer is simple; vary your diet, selecting potatoes one day and green vegetables the next.

And for Pleasure . . .

Variety is not only important for your health. It also enables you to enjoy new taste experiences. If you make your own bread, try adding a little buckwheat flour to the dough; another time, replace some of the water with partly skimmed milk. When you cook rice, treat yourself to the luxury of adding a handful of wild rice to the casserole or cook the rice in chicken stock made from a leftover carcass. Such small changes help to prevent your diet from becoming monotonous.

You can dress up the same recipes in different ways to suit the occasion. A plain shepherd's pie can be transformed into a festive meal simply by serving small cheese soufflés as starters. Steamed spinach can be made into a creamy soup or served with homemade mayonnaise, which eliminates the slightly bitter taste not appreciated by everyone. Use sauces to add variety as well; they provide an easy way to improvise on the same recipe. Use color skillfully—the addition of one or two brightly colored foods can turn an ordinary meal into an appetizing treat.

Vegetable Paella

Ingredients

250 mL (1 cup) brown rice
500 mL (2 cups) hot chicken
stock

15 mL (1 tablespoon) oil
8 Brussel sprouts
2 onions, thinly sliced
2 cloves garlic, crushed

1 green pepper, diced
1 red pepper, diced
2 tomatoes, peeled and
quartered
30 mL (2 tablespoons)
parsley, chopped
pinch saffron
salt and pepper to taste

Level of Difficulty	
Preparation Time	20 min
Cost per Serving	$
Number of Servings	4
Nutritional Value	170 calories 6.8 g protein 1.7 mg iron
Food Exchanges	3 vegetable exchanges 1 bread exchange 1/2 fat exchange
Cooking Time	42 min
Standing Time	3 min
Power Level	100%, 70%
Write Your Cooking Time Here	

Method

— Pour the chicken stock
  into a dish and add the
  rice; cover and cook at
  100% for 5 minutes.
— Reduce the power level to
  70% and continue to cook
  for 20 to 25 minutes; set
  aside.
— Pour the oil into another
  dish and add all the
  vegetables except the
  tomatoes; cover and cook
  at 100% for 6 to 7
  minutes, stirring once.
— Add the tomatoes and mix
  well; cover and allow to
  stand for 3 minutes.
— Add the parsley, saffron
  and the cooked rice;
  season to taste.
— Leave uncovered and cook
  at 100% for 3 to 5
  minutes, stirring once,
  and serve.

Chinese Beef

Level of Difficulty	🍴🍴
Preparation Time	20 min*
Cost per Serving	**$**
Number of Servings	2
Nutritional Value	410 calories 48.3 g protein 8 mg iron
Food Exchanges	4-1/2 oz meat 1 vegetable exchange 1 fat exchange
Cooking Time	4 min
Standing Time	3 min
Power Level	100%
Write Your Cooking Time Here	

* The meat should be left to marinate for 12 hours before cooking.

Ingredients
340 g (12 oz) round steak
45 mL (3 tablespoons) sesame oil
10 mL (2 teaspoons) lemon juice
30 g (1 oz) fresh ginger, thinly sliced
1 clove garlic, crushed
2 sticks celery, cut into thin strips
1 red pepper, cut into thin strips
6 green onions, thinly sliced
340 g (12 oz) bean sprouts

Method
— Cut the round steak into thin strips and set aside.
— Combine the sesame oil, lemon juice, ginger and garlic in a bowl and add the meat.
— Mix well, cover and refrigerate for 12 hours, stirring several times.
— Add the strips of celery and red pepper and the green onions; mix well.
— Preheat a browning dish at 100% for 7 minutes.
— Sauté all the ingredients and add the bean sprouts.
— Cover and cook at 100% for 3 to 4 minutes, stirring once during the cooking time.
— Allow to stand for 3 minutes before serving.

This recipe can be put together in less than half an hour. Here are the ingredients that you must assemble to prepare it.

Place the meat in the refrigerator in a covered bowl to absorb the flavor of the marinade of sesame oil, lemon juice, ginger and garlic.

Sauté the mixture of meat and vegetables and then add the bean sprouts. Proceed to the final stage of cooking.

Lentil and Ground Beef Casserole

Level of Difficulty	▲▲▲
Preparation Time	15 min
Cost per Serving	$
Number of Servings	4
Nutritional Value	270 calories 22.7 g protein 4 mg iron
Food Exchanges	3 oz meat 2 vegetable exchanges
Cooking Time	21 min
Standing Time	5 min
Power Level	100%, 70%
Write Your Cooking Time Here	

Ingredients
500 mL (2 cups) brown lentils, cooked
225 g (8 oz) lean ground beef
2 cloves garlic, chopped
1 onion, chopped
1 green pepper, chopped
15 mL (1 tablespoon) butter
3 tomatoes, peeled, chopped and drained
5 mL (1 teaspoon) thyme
2 mL (1/2 teaspoon) salt
pepper to taste
50 mL (1/4 cup) Parmesan cheese, grated

Method
— Put the garlic, onion, green pepper and butter in a dish; cover and cook at 100% for 3 to 4 minutes, stirring once during the cooking time.
— Add the ground beef and cook at 100% for 3 to 4 minutes, stirring with a fork to break up the meat twice during the cooking time.
— Add the tomatoes, thyme, salt and pepper.
— Cover and cook at 100% for 4 minutes, stirring once halfway through the cooking time to break up the tomatoes.
— Add the lentils, cover again and reduce the power level to 70%.
— Cook for 7 to 9 minutes, stirring once during the cooking time.
— Sprinkle with the Parmesan cheese and put the cover back on.
— Allow to stand for 5 minutes before serving.

Assemble the above ingredients to make this tasty dish.

Use a fork to break up the meat twice during the cooking time to ensure that it cooks evenly.

Since the lentils are already cooked, add them just before the final stage of cooking.

Veal and Vegetable Loaf

Level of Difficulty	🍴
Preparation Time	15 min
Cost per Serving	**$**
Number of Servings	6
Nutritional Value	259 calories 24.5 g protein 3.6 mg iron
Food Exchanges	3 oz meat 1 vegetable exchange
Cooking Time	24 min
Standing Time	5 min
Power Level	100%, 50%
Write Your Cooking kime Here	🍎

Ingredients
675 g (1-1/2 lb) ground veal
1 onion, finely chopped
250 mL (1 cup) carrots, grated
125 mL (1/2 cup) fresh parsley, chopped
1 egg, beaten
10 mL (2 teaspoons) powdered chicken concentrate
2 mL (1/2 teaspoon) sage
2 mL (1/2 teaspoon) savory
2 mL (1/2 teaspoon) pepper
5 mL (1 teaspoon) salt

Method
— Put all the ingredients into a large bowl and mix well.
— Place the mixture in a loaf pan.
— Press the surface gently to exclude any air bubbles.
— Cook at 100% for 5 minutes.
— Reduce the power level to 50% and continue to cook for 15 to 19 minutes, giving the dish a half-turn halfway through the cooking time.
— Allow to stand for 5 minutes before serving.

Ham Meatballs

Level of Difficulty	🍴
Preparation Time	20 min
Cost per Serving	$
Number of Servings	6
Nutritional Value	356 calories 80 g protein 43.5 mg iron
Food Exchanges	4 oz meat 1 fruit exchange
Cooking Time	10 min (plus 2 x 4 min)
Standing Time	2 x 3 min
Power Level	70%
Write Your Cooking Time Here	

Ingredients
750 mL (3 cups) cooked ham, chopped
125 mL (1/2 cup) celery, finely chopped
15 mL (1 tablespoon) onion, grated
5 mL (1 teaspoon) prepared mustard
30 mL (2 tablespoons) pineapple juice
1 egg, beaten
125 mL (1/2 cup) bran cereal, crushed
12 slices pineapple

Method
— In a large bowl, combine all the ingredients except the pineapple slices and mix well.
— Shape the mixture into 12 meatballs.
— Arrange the meatballs in a circle on a bacon rack.
— Cook at 70% for 10 minutes, giving the rack a half-turn after 5 minutes.
— Remove the meatballs and set aside. Arrange 6 slices of pineapple on the bacon rack and place 1 meatball in the center of each pineapple slice; cook at 70% for 4 minutes, or until the meatballs are done, giving the rack a half-turn after 2 minutes.
— Allow to stand for 3 minutes.
— Arrange the remaining 6 meatballs on the remaining pineapple slices and repeat the cooking procedure.

Assemble these few ingredients to make this unpretentious but tasty dish.

For the final stage of cooking, arrange the meatballs on the pineapple slices and cook six at a time.

MICROTIPS

To Make a Meal for One

Divide the recipe for ham meatballs into individual portions and freeze them separately. When you want to eat them, simply defrost the number of portions needed in the microwave oven 10 minutes before your meal.

Pita Sandwiches
with Lamb Meatballs

Level of Difficulty	
Preparation Time	15 min
Cost per Serving	$
Number of Servings	4
Nutritional Value	416 calories 29.6 g protein 36.5 g carbohydrate
Food Exchanges	3 oz meat 2 bread exchanges 1 vegetable exchange 1 fat exchange
Cooking Time	18 min 30 s
Standing Time	3 min
Power Level	70%, 100%
Write Your Cooking Time Here	

Ingredients
4 rounds of pita bread
450 g (1 lb) ground lamb
1 clove garlic, chopped
5 mL (1 teaspoon) ground coriander
salt and pepper to taste
30 mL (2 tablespoons) butter
1 green pepper, diced
1 red pepper, diced
2 green onions, thinly sliced

Method
— In a bowl combine the ground lamb, garlic and coriander; mix well and season to taste.
— Shape into small meatballs.
— Arrange the meatballs on a bacon rack.
— Cook at 70% for 8 to 10 minutes, giving the rack a half-turn halfway through the cooking time; set aside.
— Put the butter, diced peppers and green onions in a dish; cook at 100% for 4 to 5 minutes, stirring once during the cooking time.
— Add the meatballs, cover and cook at 100% for 2 minutes to reheat them.
— Allow to stand, covered, for 3 minutes.
— Cut each pita round into two and wrap each in a piece of paper towel; heat at 70% for 1-1/2 minutes.
— Fill each pita half with the meatball and vegetable mixture and serve.

Begin by assembling these ingredients to make a truly wonderful snack.

Add the cooked meatballs to the mixture of butter, diced peppers and green onions.

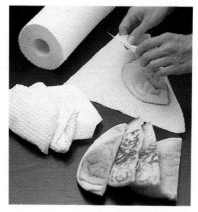

Wrap each pita half in paper towel and heat through before filling with the meatball mixture.

71

Coquilles Saint-Jacques

Level of Difficulty	
Preparation Time	15 min
Cost per Serving	$ $ $
Number of Servings	4
Nutritional Value	242 calories 26 g protein 297 mg calcium
Food Exchanges	3 oz meat 1/2 bread exchange
Cooking Time	16 min
Standing Time	2 min
Power Level	100%
Write Your Cooking Time Here	

Ingredients
2 128 mL (4-1/2 oz) cans shrimp
1 225 mL (8 oz) can lobster meat, drained and flaked
10 mL (2 teaspoons) butter
250 mL (1 cup) mushrooms, thinly sliced
250 mL (1 cup) court bouillon
250 mL (1 cup) 2% milk
75 mL (1/3 cup) flour
salt and pepper to taste
75 mL (1/3 cup) breadcrumbs
75 mL (1/3 cup) Parmesan cheese, grated

Method
— Put the butter in a dish and add the mushrooms; cover and cook at 100% for 3 to 4 minutes.
— Add the court bouillon and half the milk.
— Heat at 100% for 4 to 5 minutes, but do not allow the mixture to boil.
— Dissolve the flour in the remaining milk, mixing well to form a smooth paste, and add to the heated mixture, stirring with a whisk as you do so.
— Cook at 100% for 2 to 3 minutes, or until the mixture thickens, stirring twice during the cooking time.
— Season to taste.
— Add the shrimp and lobster meat to the sauce and stir gently.
— Place an equal amount in 4 scallop shells.
— Combine the breadcrumbs with the Parmesan cheese and sprinkle over the scallop shells.
— Reheat at 100% for 3 to 4 minutes, turning the shells once during the reheating time.
— Allow to stand for 2 minutes before serving.

This delicious dish is always popular and will delight seafood lovers. Assemble these ingredients before you begin to cook.

Stirring with a whisk, blend the mixture of flour and milk into the cooked mushrooms, butter, court bouillon and milk.

Add the shrimp and lobster meat to the sauce and pour the mixture into 4 scallop shells.

Shrimp Creole

Level of Difficulty	🍴
Preparation Time	20 min
Cost per Serving	$ $
Number of Servings	4
Nutritional Value	324 calories 29.8 g protein 4.9 mg iron
Food Exchanges	3 oz meat 1 vegetable exchange 1 bread exchange 1 fat exchange
Cooking Time	27 min
Standing Time	5 min
Power Level	100%, 70%
Write Your Cooking Time Here	

Ingredients
450 g (1 lb) shrimp, cooked and shelled
250 mL (1 cup) long grain rice
500 mL (2 cups) hot water
15 mL (1 tablespoon) parsley, chopped
30 mL (2 tablespoons) butter
2 sticks celery, diced
2 onions, chopped
1 green pepper, diced
2 cloves garlic, crushed
375 mL (1-1/2 cups) tomatoes, peeled, chopped and drained
15 mL (1 tablespoon) Worcestershire sauce
salt and pepper to taste

Method
— Put the rice and hot water in a dish; cover and cook at 100% for 5 minutes.
— Reduce the power level to 70% and continue to cook for 10 minutes.
— Add the parsley, cover and allow to stand for 5 minutes.
— Put the butter, celery, onions, green pepper and garlic in another dish; cover and cook at 100% for 4 to 5 minutes, stirring once.
— Add the tomatoes and the Worcestershire sauce; season to taste.
— Add the shrimp, cover and cook at 70% for 5 to 7 minutes, stirring once.
— Serve on a bed of rice.

Pilaf of Haddock

Level of Difficulty	🍴🔪
Preparation Time	15 min
Cost per Serving	$
Number of Servings	4
Nutritional Value	188 calories 12.9 g protein 1-1/2 mg iron
Food Exchanges	1.5 oz meat 1/2 vegetable exchange 1 bread exchange
Cooking Time	43 min
Standing Time	5 min
Power Level	100%, 70%
Write Your Cooking Time Here	🍎✏️

Ingredients
225 g (8 oz) haddock fillets, cut into pieces
15 mL (1 tablespoon) butter
1 onion, chopped
zest of 1 lemon, grated
2 mL (1/2 teaspoon) turmeric
250 mL (1 cup) brown rice
750 mL (3 cups) hot water
125 mL (1/2 cup) frozen peas
15 mL (1 tablespoon) dried parsley

Method
— Put the butter and onion in a dish; cover and cook at 100% for 2 minutes, stirring once during the cooking time.
— Add the lemon zest, turmeric, rice and hot water.
— Cook covered at 100% for 5 minutes and stir.
— Reduce the power level to 70% and continue to cook for 25 to 30 minutes, or until the rice is done.
— Add the haddock and peas; cover and cook at 100% for 4 to 6 minutes, gently stirring once during the cooking time.
— Sprinkle with parsley and allow to stand for 5 minutes before serving.

You will save yourself time and trouble by assembling all these ingredients before you begin to cook.

Stir the rice after it has cooked for 5 minutes and continue to cook as directed in the recipe.

Add the haddock and peas before the final stage of cooking.

Scallops with Vegetables

Level of Difficulty	🍴
Preparation Time	20 min
Cost per Serving	$ $
Number of Servings	4
Nutritional Value	229 calories 25-1/2 g protein 4.4 mg iron
Food Exchanges	2.5 oz meat 2 vegetable exchanges 1/2 fat exchange
Cooking Time	14 min
Standing Time	5 min
Power Level	100%, 70%
Write Your Cooking Time Here	

Ingredients
400 g (14 oz) scallops
30 mL (2 tablespoons) oil
1 clove garlic, cut into two
2 carrots, thinly sliced on the diagonal
500 mL (2 cups) broccoli flowerets
1 green pepper, thinly sliced
2 green onions, thinly sliced
250 mL (1 cup) cabbage, thinly sliced
500 mL (2 cups) bean sprouts
75 mL (1/3 cup) water
15 mL (1 tablespoon) soy sauce
5 mL (1 teaspoon) cornstarch

Method
— Preheat a browning dish at 100% for 7 minutes, add the oil and heat at 100% for 30 seconds.
— Sauté the garlic, carrots, broccoli, green pepper, green onions and cabbage.
— Cover and cook at 100% for 5 minutes, stirring once during the cooking time.
— Add the scallops and cover again.
— Reduce the power level to 70% and cook for 5 to 7 minutes, stirring once during the cooking time.
— Add the bean sprouts, cover and allow to stand for 5 minutes.
— Mix the water and soy sauce with the cornstarch; add to the vegetables and scallops and cook at 100% for 1 to 2 minutes, stirring once during the cooking.
— Remove the garlic before serving.

This pleasing combination of vegetables, with scallops, makes a highly nutritious dish.

MICROTIPS

How To Choose Scallops

When you buy scallops buy them shelled and select those with creamy white flesh, which is an indication of freshness. If possible, ask for bay scallops of the marine variety as they are usually the most tender and have a very delicate flavor.

Make Your Desserts More Nutritious

Add nutrients to cereal-based desserts by adding a few spoonfuls of wheat germ to the dough.

Salmon with Dill Sauce

Level of Difficulty	
Preparation Time	10 min
Cost per Serving	$ $
Number of Servings	4
Nutritional Value	155 calories 21.3 g protein 5.6 g lipids
Food Exchanges	3 oz meat
Cooking Time	9 min
Standing Time	4 min
Power Level	70%
Write Your Cooking Time Here	

Ingredients
4 salmon steaks
30 mL (2 tablespoons) water
pepper to taste

Sauce:
30 mL (2 tablespoons) fresh
dill, chopped
15 mL (1 teaspoon) fresh
parsley, chopped
125 mL (1/2 cup) cottage
cheese
30 mL (2 tablespoons) plain
yoghurt
salt and pepper to taste

Method
— Put the salmon steaks in a
dish, sprinkle with the
water and season with
pepper to taste.
— Cover and cook at 70%
for 7 to 9 minutes, giving
the dish a half-turn
halfway through the
cooking time.
— Allow to stand for 4
minutes.
— To make the sauce, mix
the dill and parsley in a
blender for a few seconds,
add the cottage cheese and
yoghurt and blend until
smooth; season to taste.
Heat the sauce carefully,
not allowing it to boil.
— Serve the salmon steaks
topped with the sauce.

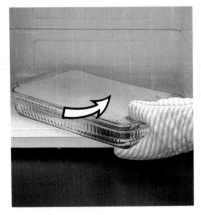

Begin by assembling all the ingredients required for this recipe, which blends the delicate flavor of salmon with that of sweet smelling dill.

Cover the salmon steaks and cook at 70% for 7 to 9 minutes.

Give the dish a half-turn halfway through the cooking time so that the steaks cook evenly.

Linguine with Shrimps and Tomatoes

Level of Difficulty	
Preparation Time	15 min
Cost per Serving	$ $
Number of Servings	4
Nutritional Value	383 calories 19.9 g protein 2.7 mg iron
Food Exchanges	2 oz meat 1 vegetable exchange 2 bread exchanges 1 fat exchange
Cooking Time	38 min
Standing Time	None
Power Level	100%
Write Your Cooking Time Here	

Ingredients
340 g (12 oz) linguine
225 g (8 oz) shrimps, shelled
1 398 mL (14 oz) can tomatoes, chopped
15 mL (1 tablespoon) oil
1 onion, chopped
2 cloves garlic, chopped
1 zucchini, grated
125 mL (1/2 cup) white wine
30 mL (2 tablespoons) parsley
salt and pepper to taste
5 mL (1 teaspoon) salt
5 mL (1 teaspoon) oil
1 L (4 cups) boiling water

Method
— Put the oil, onion, garlic and zucchini in a deep dish; cover and cook at 100% for 3 minutes, stirring once.
— Add the tomatoes, white wine and parsley and season to taste.
— Leave uncovered and cook at 100% for 15 to 20 minutes, stirring twice during the cooking time.
— Add the shrimps and continue to cook at 100% for 4 to 6 minutes.
— Cover and set aside.
— Prepare the pasta by pouring boiling water into a rectangular dish and adding the salt, oil and linguine; cook at 100% for 7 to 9 minutes, stirring twice during the cooking time.
— Drain the pasta and set aside.
— Reheat the shrimp and tomato mixture and spoon over the linguine before serving.

MICROTIPS

Pasta: Different Flavors but Similar Nutrients

It is fun to experiment with different types of pasta. A dish of spinach fettuccine served with a tarragon and tomato sauce tastes quite different from one made with buckwheat noodles and served with a rosemary-flavored sauce. Nevertheless, both dishes have about the same nutritional value.

Desserts

Desserts mean sugar, and sugar usually means refined sugar. At least, this is certainly the impression you get from reading restaurant menus and shopping for baked goods at the supermarket. Nothing, however, could be further from the truth. Fruit dishes, for example, make excellent desserts and are much better for your health than a slice of rich gâteau.

Would you really like to do yourself a favor? The next time you go shopping, explore the fruit section. You will find an increasing range of exotic fruits such as mangoes, Japanese pears and kiwi fruit, which are delicious either on their own or as part of a more elaborate dessert. Do you think that whole pineapples are expensive? Compare the price with that of a package of tiny cakes and you will find that the pineapple is less of a luxury than you thought.

With these thoughts in mind we offer the following selection of desserts to provide a finale to this volume. You will find ideas for snacks and desserts that make the most of fruit. Many of these recipes also feature whole grain cereals that are good for you. Fruit Tart, Wheat Germ Muffins, Apricot Cookies, Glazed Pears and Tofu Cheesecake are only some of our suggestions that are nutritious as well as delicious. It is still essential that any excess be avoided but, as these desserts provide real nutrients such as vitamins and fiber, there is no need to avoid them altogether.

People who have already made the switch to healthy eating know very well that refined sugar is the number one health threat and also the main cause of tooth decay; they are perfectly happy with healthy desserts that are every bit as tempting. Once you have tried a few, you will find that you no longer fancy the sugar-rich desserts that you used to crave on sight.

However, if you are one of those people who is not able to countenance such a dramatic change in your diet, you can make some compromises. Begin by preparing your favorite recipes with a reduced amount of sugar. You will slowly find yourself able to make do with a good deal less and will even eventually opt for a date square rather than Charlotte Russe. You, too, will discover with pleasure that a great dessert can also be healthy and nutritious.

Orange Muffins

Level of Difficulty	
Preparation Time	15 min
Cost per Serving	$
Number of Servings	12 muffins
Nutritional Value	99 calories 3 g protein 13.9 g carbohydrate
Food Exchanges	1 bread exchange 1/2 fat exchange
Cooking Time	2 x 2 min
Standing Time	2 x 2 min
Power Level	90%
Write Your Cooking Time Here	

Ingredients

50 mL (1/4 cup) orange juice
175 mL (3/4 cup) whole wheat flour
125 mL (1/2 cup) all purpose flour
30 mL (2 tablespoons) sugar
15 mL (1 tablespoon) baking powder
2 mL (1/2 teaspoon) salt
1 mL (1/4 teaspoon) baking soda
75 mL (1/3 cup) wheat germ
30 mL (2 tablespoons) raisins
15 mL (1 tablespoon) orange zest
1 egg
125 mL (1/2 cup) skim milk
45 mL (3 tablespoons) melted butter

Method

— In a large bowl combine both types of flour, the sugar, baking powder, salt and baking soda.
— Add the wheat germ, raisins and orange zest; set aside.
— Beat the egg and add the milk, orange juice and melted butter; add to the dry ingredients and mix just enough to bind the batter.
— Line a 6 cup muffin pan with no. 75 paper cases.
— Fill each cup just two thirds full with the batter.
— Place the pan on a rack in the oven and cook at 90% for 1-1/2 to 2 minutes, giving the pan a half-turn after 1 minute.
— Allow to stand for 2 minutes to finish off the cooking.
— Prepare 6 more muffins and cook in the same way.

At coffee-break time or for dessert, these muffins are always popular. Here are the ingredients required to make them.

Add the wheat germ, raisins and orange zest to the mixture of flour, sugar, baking powder, salt and baking soda.

Add the wet ingredients to the mixture of dry ingredients and mix just enough to bind the batter.

87

Wheat Germ Muffins

Level of Difficulty	🍴
Preparation Time	10 min
Cost per Serving	**$**
Number of Servings	12 muffins
Nutritional Value	109 calories 11.6 g carbohydrate 10.1 mg iron
Food Exchanges	1 bread exchange 1/2 fat exchange
Cooking Time	2 x 1-1/2 min
Standing Time	2 x 2 min
Power Level	90%
Write Your Cooking Time Here	

Ingredients
150 mL (2/3 cup) wheat germ
150 mL (2/3 cup) all purpose flour
150 mL (2/3 cup) whole wheat flour
15 mL (1 tablespoon) baking powder
3 mL (3/4 teaspoon) salt
45 mL (3 tablespoons) sugar
1 egg
175 mL (3/4 cup) milk
50 mL (1/4 cup) melted shortening

Method
— Sift both types of flour, the baking powder and salt into a large bowl.
— Add the wheat germ and sugar and set aside.
— In another bowl beat the egg, add the milk and shortening and mix well. Add to the dry ingredients, mixing just enough to bind the batter.
— Line a 6 cup muffin pan with no. 75 paper cases.
— Fill each cup just two thirds full with the batter.
— Place the pan on a rack in the oven and cook at 90% for 1-1/2 minutes, giving the pan a half-turn after 45 seconds.
— Allow to stand for 2 minutes to finish off the cooking.
— Prepare the cook the other 6 muffins in the same way.

Assemble all the ingredients for these moist and nutritious muffins. They are quick and easy to prepare.

For the proper consistency, begin by sifting the two types of flour, the baking powder and salt into a large bowl.

Line a 6 cup muffin pan with no. 75 paper cases. Fill each just two thirds full with the batter.

Glazed Pears

Level of Difficulty	🍴🍴 🍴🍴
Preparation Time	20 min*
Cost per Serving	$
Number of Servings	4
Nutritional Value	131 calories 32.8 g carbohydrate 16.4 mg Vitamin C
Food Exchanges	2 fruit exchanges
Cooking Time	11 min
Standing Time	None
Power Level	70%, 100%
Write Your Cooking Time Here	

* The pears should be allowed to cool between the two cooking periods and chilled in the refrigerator before serving.

Ingredients
4 ripe pears
175 mL (3/4 cup) red grape juice
8 cloves
2 cinnamon sticks, 2.5 cm (1 inch) long
5 mL (1 teaspoon) arrowroot dissolved in 45 mL (3 tablespoons) cold water

Method
— Cut a thin slice from the base of each pear, so that they stand upright.
— Peel the pears, leaving the stalks intact.
— Remove the core by cutting upwards from the base, so as not to break the stalks.
— Stand the pears upright in a dish; add the grape juice, cloves and cinnamon.
— Cover and cook at 70% for 5 to 7 minutes, giving the dish a half-turn halfway through the cooking time.
— Allow the pears to cool in their liquid, basting them several times.
— Gently remove the pears and set them aside.
— Strain the liquid and cook at 100% for 2 to 3 minutes.
— Add the dissolved arrowroot to the liquid, stirring constantly.
— Continue to cook at 100% for 1 minute, stirring after 30 seconds and again at the end of the cooking time.
— Baste the pears with the resulting sauce and refrigerate before serving.

This sophisticated dessert is just perfect for special occasions. First assemble these few ingredients.

Cut a thin slice from the base of each pear, so that they stand upright.

MICROTIPS

To Prevent Pears from Turning Brown

Pears brown very quickly once they are cut. To avoid this problem when you want to use them in a fruit salad or as a garnish, simply sprinkle them with a little lemon juice.

Fruit Tart

Level of Difficulty	🍴
Preparation Time	20 min*
Cost per Serving	**$**
Number of Servings	8
Nutritional Value	230 calories 5.2 g protein 33.9 mg calcium
Food Exchanges	1-1/2 bread exchanges 1 fruit exchange 1 fat exchange
Cooking Time	9 min 30 s
Standing Time	None
Power Level	100%, 70%
Write Your Cooking Time Here	🍎✏️

* This fruit tart should be chilled before serving.

Ingredients
500 mL (2 cups) blueberries
500 mL (2 cups) peaches, peeled and sliced
45 mL (3 tablespoons) flour
15 mL (1 tablespoon) lemon juice
10 mL (2 teaspoons) cinnamon
2 mL (1/2 teaspoon) nutmeg
30 mL (2 tablespoons) butter
45 mL (3 tablespoons) honey
500 mL (2 cups) rolled oats
125 mL (1/2 cup) almonds, sliced

Method
— Mix the blueberries with the peaches in a bowl and add 15 mL (1 tablespoon) of the flour, the lemon juice, half the cinnamon and the nutmeg.
— Grease a flan dish, arrange the fruit mixture in it and set aside.
— Put the butter in a dish and heat at 100% for 1 minute until it melts; add the honey, heat at 100% for 30 seconds and set aside.
— In another dish mix the rolled oats and almonds with the remaining cinnamon and flour; add the honey and butter mixture and stir.
— Spoon the mixture over the fruit and spread evenly.
— Press the surface gently to make it smooth.
— Place the dish on a rack in the oven and cook at 70% for 6 to 8 minutes, giving the dish a half-turn halfway through the cooking time.
— Allow to cool and chill in the refrigerator before serving.

Assemble these ingredients for a healthy dessert that will delight your guests.

Mix the blueberries and peaches together and add 15 mL (1 tablespoon) of the flour, the lemon juice, 5 mL (1 teaspoon) of the cinnamon and the nutmeg.

Press the surface of the tart gently to make it smooth and proceed with the final stage of cooking.

Scones

Level of Difficulty	🍴
Preparation Time	20 min
Cost per Serving	**$**
Number of Servings	12 scones
Nutritional Value	111 calories 14.6 g carbohydrate 72.4 mg calcium
Food Exchanges	1/4 milk exchange 1 bread exchange 1/2 fat exchange
Cooking Time	2 x 1 min
Standing Time	2 x 2 min
Power Level	90%
Write Your Cooking Time Here	

Ingredients
425 mL (1-3/4 cups) whole wheat flour
15 mL (1 tablespoon) baking powder
pinch salt
pinch cayenne pepper
45 mL (3 tablespoons) butter
250 mL (1 cup) skim milk
60 g (2 oz) cheddar cheese, finely grated

Method
— Mix all the ingredients together in a bowl to make a smooth dough.
— Knead gently and then roll out to 1.5 cm (1/2 inch) thick.
— Cut 12 rounds out of the dough with a cookie cutter.
— Arrange 6 scones on a plate and place on a rack in the oven; cook at 90% for 45 to 60 seconds, giving the dish a half-turn halfway through the cooking time.
— Allow to stand for 2 minutes to finish off the cooking.
— Cook the remaining 6 scones in the same way.

These delicious little scones will be a resounding success at coffee-break time. Here are the ingredients to be assembled in order to make them.

Mix all the ingredients together
to make a smooth dough.

Knead the dough gently and
then roll it out to 1.5 cm
(1/2 inch) thick. Using a cookie
cutter, cut 12 rounds out of the
dough.

Place 6 scones on a plate and
cook on a rack in the oven, with
the power level at 90%, for 45
to 60 seconds. Give the dish a
half-turn halfway through the
cooking time.

Oranges in Wine

Level of Difficulty	🍴🍴
Preparation Time	15 min*
Cost per Serving	$ $
Number of Servings	6
Nutritional Value	124 calories 28.2 g carbohydrate 71.2 mg Vitamin C
Food Exchanges	2 fruit exchanges
Cooking Time	10 min
Standing Time	20 min
Power Level	100%, 70%
Write Your Cooking Time Here	

* The oranges must be refrigerated for 2 hours before serving.

Ingredients
6 oranges
zest of 2 oranges, cut into thin strips
125 mL (1/2 cup) dry white wine
125 mL (1/2 cup) water
50 mL (1/4 cup) sugar
3 cloves
1 cinnamon stick
15 mL (1 tablespoon) lemon juice

Method
— Peel and slice the oranges and remove any seeds.
— Put the orange slices with the orange zest in a dish and set aside.
— Put all the other ingredients into a bowl and mix well.
— Cook at 100% for 4 to 5 minutes and stir.
— Reduce the power level to 70% and continue to cook for 4 to 5 minutes longer, stirring once during the cooking time.
— Pour the syrup over the orange slices.
— Allow to stand for 20 minutes.
— Refrigerate for 2 hours, remove the cinnamon stick and the cloves and serve.

This dessert is very quick to make and is suitable for any occasion. Begin by assembling these ingredients.

Peel and slice the oranges and remove any seeds.

Pour the cooked syrup over the orange slices and allow to stand for 20 minutes.

Refrigerate for 2 hours, remove the cinnamon and cloves and serve.

Apricot Cookies

Level of Difficulty	🍴
Preparation Time	20 min
Cost per Serving	$
Number of Servings	36 cookies (18 servings)
Nutritional Value	116 calories 9.5 g carbohydrate 7 mg iron
Food Exchanges	1/2 fruit exchange 1 bread exchange
Cooking Time	2 x 1-1/2 min
Standing Time	2 x 3 min
Power Level	90%
Write Your Cooking Time Here	

Ingredients
125 mL (1/2 cup) dried apricots, chopped
125 mL (1/2 cup) sunflower oil
50 mL (1/4 cup) brown sugar
1 egg
175 mL (3/4 cup) whole wheat flour
5 mL (1 teaspoon) baking soda
2 mL (1/2 teaspoon) cinnamon
2 mL (1/2 teaspoon) salt
250 mL (1 cup) rolled oats

Method
— Combine the oil and the brown sugar, whisk until foamy; add the egg, whisk again and set aside.
— Sift the flour, baking soda, cinnamon and salt into the liquid mixture and beat with a wooden spoon.
— Add the rolled oats and the apricots and mix.
— Use half the batter to shape 18 cookies and place them on a cookie sheet.
— Place the sheet on a rack in the oven and cook at 90% for 1-1/2 minutes, giving the sheet a half-turn halfway through the cooking time.
— Allow to stand for 3 minutes.
— Repeat the preceding 3 steps with the remainder of the batter.

Tofu Cheesecake

Level of Difficulty	1
Preparation Time	10 min*
Cost per Serving	1
Number of Servings	8
Nutritional Value	180 calories 8.4 g protein 27.6 g carbohydrate
Food Exchanges	1 fruit exchange 1 milk exchange
Cooking Time	11 min
Standing Time	None
Power Level	70%
Write Your Cooking Time Here	

* This cheesecake should be chilled before serving.

Ingredients
450 g (1 lb) tofu, drained
75 mL (1/3 cup) white sugar
3 egg whites
175 mL (3/4 cup) sweetened condensed milk
5 mL (1 teaspoon) lemon juice
5 mL (1 teaspoon) lemon zest
1 drop almond essence
24 apricot halves, drained

Method
— Put all the ingredients except the apricots into a blender.
— Purée for a few seconds.
— Distribute the mixture in a greased flan dish.
— Arrange the apricot halves on top of the mixture.
— Place the dish on a rack in the oven and cook at 70% for 9 to 11 minutes, giving the dish a half-turn halfway through the cooking time.
— Allow to cool and refrigerate before serving.

Here are the ingredients required to make a tofu cheesecake with a delicate flavor that is sure to win compliments.

Put all the ingredients except the apricots into a blender and purée for a few seconds.

Distribute the tofu mixture in a greased flan dish and arrange the apricot halves on top.

Place the dish on a rack in the oven and cook at 70% for 9 to 11 minutes, giving the dish a half-turn halfway through the cooking time.

Your Healthy Eating Plan

Breakfast	Lunch	Supper
Whole wheat bread 1/2 grapefruit Cheese Coffee, tea or milk	Cream of Rutabaga Soup Croque-monsieur Fresh fruit Coffee, tea or milk	Tomato juice Chicken with Yoghurt Broccoli Coconut pie Coffee, tea or milk
Orange Muffin Fruit yoghurt Coffee, tea or milk	Vichyssoise Country-style omelette Apricot Cookies Coffee, tea or milk	Cucumber salad Ham Meatballs Rice pilaf Fresh fruit Coffee, tea or milk
Orange juice English muffin Peanut butter Coffee, tea or milk	Minestrone Soup Eggplant quiche Fruit yoghurt Coffee, tea or milk	Tomatoes stuffed with alfalfa Liver Loaf Braised vegetables Creamed rice with peaches Coffee, tea or milk
Cereal with Strawberries Biscuits 30 g (1 oz) cheese Coffee, tea or milk	Green salad Pizza soufflé Stuffed peaches Coffee, tea or milk	Cucumber and Tomato Tomato Soup Whole wheat crackers Stuffed vegetable marrow Plain yoghurt with peaches Coffee, tea or milk
1/2 cantaloupe Cheese muffin Coffee, tea or milk	Barley and vegetable soup Rice and cheese loaf Carrot and celery sticks Fresh fruit Coffee, tea or milk	Lentil and tomato soup Manicotti with spinach Green salad Oranges in Wine Coffee, tea or milk
Fresh fruit cup Whole wheat toast 1 scrambled egg Coffee, tea or milk	Cauliflower soup Mexican-style pita sandwich Tomato wedges Ice cream cup Coffee, tea or milk	Tomato juice Salmon with Dill Sauce Vegetable Paella Fruit Tart Coffee, tea or milk
	Sunday Brunch Orange quarters or 1/2 grapefruit Cranberry loaf Spring omelette Coffee, tea or milk	Marinated leeks Roast veal Parsley potatoes Harvard beets Yoghurt and peach cake Coffee, tea or milk

Breakfast	Lunch	Supper
Pineapple juice Toasted bagel Cheese and ham Coffee, tea or milk	Beef Soup Whole wheat crackers Fruit yoghurt Oatmeal cookies Coffee, tea or milk	Spanish consommé Spaghetti with meat sauce Raw vegetable salad Glazed Pears Coffee, tea or milk
Orange or grapefruit juice Wheat Germ Muffin Plain yoghurt with walnuts Coffee, tea or milk	Vegetable juice Broccoli and cheese quiche Carrot salad Fresh fruit Coffee, tea or milk	Clear vegetable soup Whole wheat bread Pilaf of Haddock Glazed carrots Spinach purée Pineapple flan Coffee, tea or milk
High-fiber toast Apple purée Cheese Coffee, tea or milk	Raw vegetables Ham parmentier Melon and strawberries Coffee, tea or milk	Cream of Leek and Broccoli Soup Rice with pork and vegetables Ice cream with raspberry purée Coffee, tea or milk
Whole wheat toast Peanut butter Banana Coffee, tea or milk	Carrot Soup Noodles with tuna Spinach salad Fresh fruit cup Coffee, tea or milk	Chicken and snow pea soup Chicken with apricots Broccoli with Mushrooms Scones Coffee, tea or milk
1/2 grapefruit Oats, raisins and almonds Coffee, tea or milk	Broad bean soup Whole wheat bread and cretons Raw vegetables Fruit yoghurt Coffee, tea or milk	Crab Soup Beef sauté with orange segments Rice Lichee mousse Coffee, tea or milk
Cheese muffin Apple purée Plain yoghurt Coffee, tea or milk	Vegetable juice Grandmother's macaroni Green salad Fresh fruit Coffee, tea or milk	Greek-style mushrooms Scallops with Vegetables Brown rice Ice cream and blueberries Coffee, tea or milk
	Sunday Brunch Orange and pineapple juice Navy Beans with Pineapple Ham Whole wheat toast Coffee, tea or milk	Apple juice Roast pork with potatoes and gravy Zucchini Provençale Tofu Cheesecake Coffee, tea or milk

Food Facts

Nuts store well for a long time. They can be kept for several months in the refrigerator. To store them even longer, they may be frozen.

Triticale is a hybrid grain obtained by crossing wheat with rye. It forms a light bread dough that is high in protein.

Canadian regulations stipulate that flour mills add iron, thiamin, riboflavin and niacin to all purpose flour because these nutrients are removed in the refining process.

Three types of soya flour are available: whole or full fat, partially defatted, and completely defatted.

Oregano is a type of marjoram.

Bulrushes are edible. The white part of the stalk can be finely chopped and added to salads.

The foods that most commonly cause allergic reactions are wheat, milk, eggs, seafood and chocolate.

Vitamin K is essential to the blood-clotting process. It is found in leafy vegetables, cabbage and milk.

Asparagus is a good source of Vitamins A and C; it is also rich in calcium, phosphorus, thiamin, potassium and iron.

Broccoli is rich in Vitamin C and also contains Vitamin A, thiamin, riboflavin, calcium and iron.

The Jerusalem artichoke is also known as the Canadian artichoke.

Spinach, green cabbage, sweet potatoes, ordinary potatoes and curly green cabbage are regarded as the vegetables with the most nutritional value. They are closely followed by winter squash, broccoli and asparagus.

Over 7000 types of apples are grown in North America.

Watermelon, mango, orange and cantaloupe are considered to be the fruits with the most nutrients.

Health Food Terminology

The terminology used in the food sciences derives in part from biochemistry. Some of the words are therefore academic terms. Here is a glossary to help explaim them.

Amino acids: The basic constituents of protein. The body uses amino acids to form the proteins it needs.

Anemia: A condition in which the red blood cell count is lower than normal. The symptoms include fatigue, an increased pulse rate and breathlessness at the slightest exertion.

Anorexia: An illness characterized by a loss of appetite and often accompanied by a complete aversion to food; it is particularly common among adolescents.

Bulimia: Exaggerated feelings of hunger that accompany some physical and mental disorders.

Cellulose: The structural element of carbohydrates found in food fiber.

Cholesterol: A complex natural substance that is wax-like in appearance. It is essential to the body, especially to the brain, nervous system and cell membranes. Cholesterol also aids in the production of hormones and Vitamin D and in the digestion of fats. Although cholesterol has a reputation for being associated with heart disease, scientists have not been able to establish a clear cause-and-effect link between high blood cholesterol levels and heart disease.

Diuretic: Food or medication that stimulates the production of urine.

Fats: Fats are essential to the body and transport the fat-soluble Vitamins A, D, E and K.

Fiber: The cell wall that supports plant cells forms food fiber. It is not digested by the stomach but is partly absorbed by bacteria in the intestine. Fiber is a substance well known for preventing constipation. Fiber-rich foods include bran, dried figs, prunes and popcorn.

Fructose: A sugar found in plants.

Hyperglycemia: A condition characterized by an excessivly high blood suger level.

Hypoglycemia: A condition characterized by a low blood sugar level.

Ketogenic: A term used to describe diets containing large amounts of fat but minimal amounts of protein and carbohydrate to stimulate the production of keytone bodies, which leads to weight loss.

Lactose: The sugar found in milk.

Metabolism: The organic process that transforms digested nutrients into energy.

Niacin: A vitamin from the B group. It has a function similar to that of riboflavin and helps in the body's supply of energy.

Riboflavin: A vitamin from the B group. It helps to free the food energy in carbohydrates and fats.

Sweetner: Any substance that sweetens foods. Sugar is the sweetener that is most frequently used in cooking.

Thiamin: A vitamin from the B group. It aids in energy production, growth, the maintenance of a healthy appetite, the digestion and the functioning of the nervous system.

Trace elements: Elements that are present in the body in minute quantities and that are essential to its functioning. They include iron, zinc, iodine, copper, magnesium, chromium, molybdenum, nickel, selenium, tin, vanadium and cobalt.

Vitamins: Organic chemical substances that are essential to life and growth. Vitamins must be included in the diet because the body itself does not manufacture them in quantities sufficient to meet its needs. There are two types of vitamins: those that dissolve in fat and those that dissolve in water.

Understand What You Are Eating

You will have noticed the food chart preceding each recipe in this *Microwave Magic* series. It provides useful information about the recipe at a glance.

The first entry indicates, by one, two or three knife-and-fork symbols, whether the recipe is easy, somewhat difficult or quite difficult to prepare. The more symbols you see, the greater the cooking skills required.

The chart then gives the preparation time for the recipe in question. This time represents the approximate time needed to assemble the ingredients and the utensils, to chop any vegetables and to do the measuring, mixing and beating.

Third, we give an approximate cost for each serving. An economical meal is indicated by one dollar sign. A more elaborate meal has two dollar signs and a truly luxurious meal has three.

It is very important that you know the number of servings you will obtain from a recipe. The next entry therefore specifies this number.

We have been very careful to ensure that our recipes provide plenty of nutrients. We think it is very important for you to know the nutritional value provided by each one; the number of calories as well as the quantities of protein, minerals and other nutrients are therefore given. The way in which the ingredients have been produced and stored can affect their nutritional value dramatically, so the figures given here may not always be totally accurate.

A balanced diet should include a certain number of servings from each of the four food groups. The food exchange entry indicates the amount of meat and the number of servings of milk, bread and fruit or vegetables in the recipe for each person. It also shows the amount of fat contained in each serving.

The cooking time is clearly shown to make it easy for you to coordinate the preparation of a complete meal.

Microwave cooking continues for a short time even after the food is removed from the oven. Some recipes therefore have a specified standing time, which is essential for the food to finish cooking. So, do not be surprised if you feel that some dishes do not seem fully cooked when you take them out of the oven. The standing time will be sufficient to bring them to perfection.

It is important to set the oven controls properly. The chart therefore clearly shows the power level required for each recipe.

Try Something New!

Explore the shelves in your supermarket to find foods that are new to you. More and more exotic fruits and vegetables are becoming available; mangoes, Japanese pears and kiwi fruit are all delicious, eaten as they are or used in desserts. You will find a great variety of vegetables as well. Gone are the days when salads consisted of plain old iceberg lettuce. Today, you will find romaine lettuce, curly lettuce, escarole and endive in every supermarket. You will also find vegetables that were virtually unheard of until recent years, such as kohlrabi and alfalfa sprouts. At the cheese counter, too, you will find that cheddar must now share the limelight. Other flavorful cheeses from around the world such as Gorgonzola, Havarti, triple crème and chèvre (goat's cheese) are truly worth testing.

Conversion Chart

**Conversion Chart for the
Main Measures Used in
Cooking**

Volume
1 teaspoon............	5 mL
1 tablespoon........	15 mL
1 quart (4 cups).......	1 litre
1 pint (2 cups).......	500 mL
1/2 cup............	125 mL
1/4 cup............	50 mL

Weight
2.2 lb..........	1 kg (1000 g)
1.1 lb...............	500 g
0.5 lb...............	225 g
0.25 lb...............	115 g
1 oz.................	30 g

**Metric Equivalents
for Cooking
Temperatures**

49°C...............	120°F	120°C...............	250°F
54°C...............	130°F	135°C...............	275°F
60°C...............	140°F	150°C...............	300°F
66°C...............	150°F	160°C...............	325°F
71°C...............	160°F	180°C...............	350°F
77°C...............	170°F	190°C...............	375°F
82°C...............	180°F	200°C...............	400°F
93°C...............	200°F	220°C...............	425°F
107°C...............	225°F	230°C...............	450°F

Readers will note that, in the recipes, we give 250 mL as the
equivalent for 1 cup and 450 g as the equivalent for 1 lb and
that fractions of these measurements are even less
mathematically accurate. The reason for this is that
mathematically accurate conversions are just not practical in
cooking. Your kitchen scales are simply not accurate enough
to weigh 454 g—the true equivalent of 1 lb—and it would be
a waste of time to try. The conversions given in this series,
therefore, necessarily represent approximate equivalents, but
they will still give excellent results in the kitchen. No problems
should be encountered if you adhere to either metric or
imperial measurements throughout a recipe.

Index

MICROTIPS